D1379421

FROM BERKELEY TO
EAST BERLIN AND BACK

FROM BERKELEY TO
EAST BERLIN AND BACK

DALE VREE

Thomas Nelson Publishers
Nashville • Camden • New York

Published in Nashville, Tennessee, by Thomas Nelson, Inc. and distributed in Canada by Lawson Falle, Ltd., Cambridge, Ontario.

Printed in the United States of America.

Unless otherwise noted, the Bible version used in this publication is the King James Version of the Bible.

Scripture quotations noted NASB are from the New American Standard Bible, © The Lockman Foundation 1960, 1962, 1963, 1968, 1971, 1972, 1975, 1977, and are used by permission.

Scripture quotations noted NEB are from *The New English Bible*. © The Delegates of the Oxford University Press and the Syndics of the Cambridge University Press 1961, 1970. Reprinted by permission.

Library of Congress Cataloging in Publication Data

Vree, Dale, 1944–
  From Berkeley to East Berlin and back.

  1. Vree, Dale, 1944– . 2. Converts—Biography.
3. Communism. 4. Communism and Christianity. 5. Sexual ethics—United States. 6. Capitalism. 7. Consumption (Economics)—United States—Moral and ethical aspects.
8. United States—Moral conditons. I. Title.
BV4935.V74A34   1985   209'.2'4 [B]   85-251
ISBN 0-8407-5463-9

To Elena.
Forever.

CONTENTS

vii

ACKNOWLEDGMENTS

Parts of chapters 1 and 2 are drawn from a previous essay by the author which appeared in the November 1974 issue of *Worldview* magazine, 170 E. 64th St., New York, N.Y. 10021, with permission from the editor. Parts of chapters 3 and 4 are drawn with permission of the editor from a previous essay by the author which appeared in the April 1981 issue of *Eternity* magazine, 1716 Spruce St., Philadelphia, Pa. 19103.

Essential research for this book was made possible by a summer grant from the Earhart Foundation and by two year-long grants, one a Rockefeller Foundation Humanities Fellowship (while the author was a Visiting Scholar at the Institute of International Studies at the University of California at Berkeley) and the other a National Endowment for the Humanities Fellowship (as part of the National Fellows Program at the Hoover Institution at Stanford University).

AN EX-MARXIST
EXPOSED

At the end of the summer of 1972 I left Berkeley and arrived at Earlham College, deep in the woods of eastern Indiana, to begin teaching political science. Within days of my arrival, a reporter from the student newspaper knocked on my office door and politely asked for an interview. I agreed, and let him in.

When he asked for a detailed account of my political past, I was taken aback. *Somehow the news has leaked out,* I said to myself. Since I didn't want to seem defensive, I tried to accommodate him and answer his questions. But during the whole interview I was uneasy—a feeling that intensified when I saw the first Earlham *Post* of the school year. The story carried the blazing headline, "Former Marxist Joins Political Science Department."

I wasn't eager to identify myself that way, but now the cat was out of the bag. My discomfort was compounded when I realized that many students somehow missed the "Former" in the headline. The word got around that I was still a flaming Marxist, not that I was an ex-Marxist. Ah, the wonders of selective perception!

In the Berkeley of that era one knew not to admit to being a *former* Marxist for fear of being branded a craven sellout. In Indiana, however, I instantly became a roguish celebrity. I found out that many students were taking my classes not so much to learn about political science as to take a good, long look at the instructor. Students were delighted when I would say something revealing or outrageous. I'll never forget once saying something in front of a jam-packed, steamy undergraduate class about some exotic committee on campus, when accidentally the word *cell* popped out of my mouth instead. Before I realized what I had uttered, the class erupted with knowing hollers and prurient giggles.

Episodes like this one during my three-year stay in Indiana, plus the initial interview with the *Post* reporter, began a series of reminiscences in my mind that eventually resulted in the book you are about to read. Accordingly, the first chapters of this book are devoted to autobiography. For a host of reasons it is embarrassingly presumptuous, vain, and self-indulgent for anyone under fifty to yield to the autobiographical impulse. I must, however, beg your indulgence, for I know of no better way to speak vividly about the questionable marriage of convenience between Christianity and consumerist anti-Communism, and of beginning to expose the passionate but secretive affair that exists between capitalism and sexual freedom—liaisons that feed into the basic theme of this book: facing up to social adversity.

For us Christians, Communism and sexual freedom are occasions of social adversity. Without capitulating to either one, I wish to show how we might find the face of Christ in the midst of these occasions of adversity and, by implication, in adversity generally.

Taken together, Communism and sexual freedom represent a wrenching turn of our civilization away from Christianity. Throughout these pages I will urge Christians to respond to these challenges in a firm but wise and spiritually discerning manner, to avoid self-centered overreaction and blind panic, and to etch in our minds the warning of the Anglo-Welsh Christian poet, David Jones: "It is easy to miss Him/at the turn of a civilisation."

My unconventional perspective on social adversity is undoubtedly tied up with my participation in Berkeley's Free Speech Movement, my Marxist past, my temporary expatriation in East Germany, and my unexpected conversion to Jesus Christ in East Berlin. But the point of the autobiographical chapters is not to tell you about *me* as much as it is to tell you about *us*. Indeed, this entire book is an invitation to American and Western Christians to see ourselves and our relationship to our civilization in a new and (perhaps initially) unsettling way.

PART ONE

A PERSONAL JOURNEY

O N E

BERKELEY:
ALL THOSE YEARS AGO

Berkeley more than Paris, more than either Cambridge [Cambridge, Massachusetts, or Cambridge, England]...has now and for decades been known as the place where things begin. • *John Kenneth Galbraith*

Why did I become a Marxist in the first place? This obvious question requires an extensive answer.

I was given an evangelical Christian upbringing. And, at least at the conscious level, I was motivated by a desire to find a coherent expression of the Christian ethical life in the social realm. Even in high school, I thought that a Christian society would necessarily be a sharing one.

Moreover, I had a bias in favor of the common man, the workingman, and an aversion to the rich. My acquaintance with modern world history persuaded me that socialism was the natural ally of the common people. Hence, socialism was the point of contact between my religious inclinations and my socioeconomic sensibilities.

Why was I predisposed in favor of the proverbial common man? All four of my grandparents

17

were plebian immigrants from Holland who settled initially in the Midwest and finally in California. This generation of Dutch immigrants consisted of pleasingly uncultivated and hearty folk.

My elders were peasants, workers, adventurers, and small merchants. My father, Henry, didn't graduate from high school but finished his schooling at a trade school. He planted in me a primitive proletarian consciousness—an ability to see society from a working-class point of view—which he inherited from his father, Willem, who began his working life as a mechanic and sheet-metal pressman. My grandfather, a genuinely self-taught man, was particularly fond of Edwin Markham's poem, "The Man with the Hoe." The piece begins:

> Bowed by the weight of centuries he leans
> Upon his hoe and gazes on the ground,
> The emptiness of ages in his face,
> And on his back the burden of the world.

And it ends:

> How will it be with kingdoms and with
>   kings—
> With those who shaped him to the thing
>   he is—
> When this dumb terror shall rise to judge
>   the world,
> After the silence of the centuries?

Not surprisingly, then, my father taught me to respect the common man, his culture, his trade unions—his very commonness—and to distrust the high and the mighty and see through their pompous posturing. Dad loved to paraphrase the

18

words of Kipling for me: "If you can walk with kings, but not lose the common touch...you'll be a Man, my son!"

Dad was instructing his son, his only son. "The common touch" was the priceless lesson he tried to impart to me. And when he was dying, he was to say to me over and over again that he would rather be a mere doorkeeper in the house of the Lord than sit in the seats of the mighty.

Ironically, though, Dad had married a Dutch-American girl, Marion Wyma, who proved to have anything but proletarian consciousness. She was the daughter of a house painter/wallpaper hanger to be sure, but she was upwardly mobile. Largely through her personal drive, my immediate family rose from a lower-middle-class status to an upper-middle one within a decade.

Dad, who grew up in the ethnic sections of Chicago, was a populist Democrat. He loathed all pretension—whether caused by too much wealth, too much education, too much culture, too much striving, or too much righteousness. Like his father, Dad was a Truman-Kefauver Democrat, not a Stevenson-style Democrat (Stevenson's patricianism undoubtedly had much to do with this).

Since the Dutch-American immigrants who gravitated to the Midwest are arch-Calvinists, oriented to individual success, and heavily Republican, it is significant that my father and grandfather were such strong Democrats. The working-class issue was singularly responsible for this. I remember being informed at the young age of four that the Democrats were the party of the workingman. Nothing more needed to be said on the subject.

19

Dad and Grandpa's Democratic views were the source of tension with relatives. My maternal grandfather, himself a workingman, once announced that Dad would vote for the devil if he was running on the Democratic ticket. Dad was infuriated, but he wouldn't deny it.

For most of his life, Dad was a draftsman in the kitchen equipment field. Though he was not technically a manual worker, if a pollster had asked whether he identified himself as working class or middle class, he would certainly have responded, "working class."

Mother, who is still living, is quite the opposite. She is largely nonpolitical, but she would be happiest with a cultivated, Rockefeller-style Republican party. She probably picked up her refined preferences in the process of rising out of the tiny Dutch subculture in southern California.

The first female in our intensely patriarchal subculture to go to college, she began her career as a teacher in one of the rougher junior high schools in Los Angeles, where girls (never mind the boys!) carried knives in their hair. Through hard work and determination she eventually earned a doctorate and became a professor of music at a community college in L.A. If a pollster were to ask her if she identifies herself as working class or middle class, she would undoubtedly pick the latter.

My mother emphasized advancement through education. If it hadn't been for her, I would never have gone to college. When I wanted to take auto shop and similar courses in high school, she exploded and insisted I take precollegiate courses instead. But this emphasis coexisted uneasily with the basic mind-set I got from Dad—what Mother would probably dub the mentality of an auto mechanic. Mother succeeded in getting me into college, but she didn't succeed in teaching me or my father manners, refinement, or an appreciation for "real" culture. On these issues it was, as Dad would have said, a Mexican stand-off.

So, thanks to my mother I went to college, but thanks to my father I was ripe for Marxism once I got there. Curiously, it wasn't until I discovered Marxism and the history of the working class that I became interested in my studies and really came alive intellectually. Although neither my father nor my mother had the slightest interest in Marxism, Marxism, of all things, bridged their two worlds for me.

THE BRIDGE

During the 1963-64 academic year I was a junior at Cal-Berkeley. I was active in the Bay Area civil rights movement and the Berkeley chapter of the "Old Left" Young People's Socialist League (YPSL), then the major social democratic youth group in America. But the Berkeley YPSL split three ways that year, and I was ideologically cut adrift.

In the summer of 1964 I had a chance to visit the Soviet Union, Poland, East Germany, and Czechoslovakia and to compare those countries with social democratic Western Europe. I came to believe that Marxism-Leninism, not social democracy, was the hope of the laboring class, by which it would emancipate itself not only from capitalist exploitation but also from decadent, bourgeois culture.

In contrast to this ideal, social democratic Europe seemed just like capitalist America. Most travelers to Eastern Europe are mortified by the spartan, drab, and uniform quality of life there. I, on the other hand, was impressed. There was a sense of purpose, struggle, and militance there that appealed to me. One did not have to be told that the ostentatious and jaded bourgeoisie had been expurgated; one could actually feel it in the air.

I can remember sitting on the balcony of my room over the main street in Prague one night and feeling a profound surge of emotion. Incredibly, I felt very much at home. The next day I attended a workers' rally at which Nikita Khrushchev and various Czechoslovak leaders spoke. It wasn't a particularly auspicious event—and I didn't understand a word, of course—but I was strangely moved. Had the "man with the hoe" finally risen up to judge the world? This experience and others in Eastern Europe, plus further readings in Marxism, caused me to come back to Berkeley not as a social democrat but as a communist.

How pleasant it was to return to the Berkeley campus that fall and move right into the circle surrounding the emerging Free Speech Movement (FSM), the eruption that everyone agrees was to give substance to the theories of the embryonic New Left and ignite the entire American student movement of the midsixties and early seventies. When classes started again, of the more than 27,000 students on campus, according to sociologist William Petersen, "perhaps 200 to 300 radicals were primed for rebellion."[1] Although more of a book reader than an organizer, I suppose I was one of that small group. Arrested on December 3, 1964, for "sitting in" at Sproul Hall and resisting arrest, I managed to do my part for the cause. Locked up for twenty-four hours in a faraway jail, I returned to campus the next day feeling very much like a heroic soldier returning from a foreign war.

When the dust settled, the FSM emerged largely victorious, and people of all sorts were struggling to interpret what had happened. All agreed that the FSM was unprecedented—it had orchestrated probably the most militant, stunning, and successful series of student demonstrations in American university history. Curiosity seekers and dissidents with or without a cause began migrating to the Berkeley campus to watch or take part in hoped-for encores.

But free speech had been only a surface issue, even for members of the FSM. According to Jack Weinberg, a leading figure on the FSM Steering Committee, the roots of the FSM "go much deeper. The free-speech issue has been so readily accepted because it has become a vehicle enabling students to express their dissatisfaction with so much of university life."[2] Soon the common complaints were not speech-related at all, but rather that classes were too large and impersonal, professors were too involved in research at the expense of interaction with students, too much of the learning experience was nullified by cramming for exams and jockeying for grades, and too much emphasis was placed on preparing for vocation and not enough on self-discovery.

As two popular professors then teaching at Berkeley put it, students "come to college in search, not merely of knowledge, but of salvation."[3]

The FSM's dissatisfaction with the university reflected a more general alienation from industrial society. The salvation or meaning the student missed inside the university was not to be found outside either. According to Weinberg, the individual in society "finds it increasingly more difficult to find meaning in his job or in his life."[4] The FSM's top leader, Mario Savio, plausibly characterized society as a "consumer's paradise" that provides "no challenge" and is "simply no longer exciting."[5]

But this malaise led to curious remedies, as when Savio admitted that his reasons for journeying to Mississippi the previous summer to do civil rights work had been "selfish." "My middle-class life," he added, "had no place in society, nor it in me. It was not really a matter of fighting for constitutional rights. I needed some way to pinch myself, to assure myself that I was alive."[6] If meaninglessness was the problem, the solution was somehow to pinch oneself.

SHIFTING PREOCCUPATIONS

The FSM catalyzed a profound shift in the direction of the emerging New Left, which theretofore had paid attention only to the woes not of the working class but of the down and out, or as writer Michael Harrington put it, "the powerless, the maimed, the poor, the criminal, the junkie."[7] In one sense this represented a commendable concern for others, but the early New Left's infatuation with the down and out too often grew out of a mindless urge to scandalize conventional soci-

24

ety—and its romance with the black poor was too often grounded in the pursuit of penance for guilt feelings.

The FSM swiftly diverted attention away from these "others," not toward the regular working class but toward self. The success of the FSM signaled to the rising New Left, both nationally and internationally, that students alone and independent of any messianic lower class could change society. The FSM, an affluent white youth movement openly concerned with its own grievances, made self-preoccupation respectable for radicals. This shift began discrediting the New Left in my eyes.

Students were preoccupied with their own personal alienation, which was a tip-off to the class character of their radicalism. Only those who are so affluent as not to feel exploited economically, or who are so encapsulated in an affluent lifestyle that they have no contact with, or interest in, those who feel economic deprivation, will raise the banner of their own alienation above all other banners.

But crying about alienation served its purpose. In a country like the United States, permeated with the spirit—but not the reality—of egalitarianism, it is convenient for the powerful to pretend to be hamstrung and the rich taxed to death. Accordingly, privileged youth needed to be able to pose as just one more victimized group. And the appeal to alienation did the trick. It supplied the ideological basis for self-preoccupation, which quickly branched out into new forms of self-indulgence, from sleeping around to drug taking and then on to women's liberation and gay liberation.

Alienation is a common complaint, and it is

really a fancy word for frustration. But frustration is common to all classes. The proposed political cures for alienation—decentralization, democratization, and increased participation—had a rather diffuse focus. And as long as the working class was not the focus of attention, these cures had no obvious connection with the demand for workers' ownership and control of the major institutions of production, which is the starting point for any truly radical change in modern society.

In this situation, where an elusive ailment such as alienation had been raised as a public issue, the university was limited in what it could offer its students. It could not promise that society would listen to them. It could, however, listen to them and try to respond to their more concrete complaints. For some reason unknown to me, the structure of the university had been frequently charged with culpability for the FSM trauma. Naturally, therefore, the Berkeley campus was soon bubbling with recipes for "meaningful educational experience" and "student power."

I don't think students had given these issues much thought, but these issues served as anvils on which students could hammer out their frustrations. I was amazed by the speed with which my fellow students—radicals included—fell for the bait of educational reform. But as protest and change seemed to become ends in themselves, I was losing hope for the serious revolutionary potential of the movement, which seemed increasingly afflicted with narcissism or hypochondria or both.

Berkeley: All Those Years Ago
PURER VIRTUES

The truth is, I was quite happy in the university. I was neither grasping for meaning in life nor rebelling against industrial civilization, for Marxists are not supposed to lack meaning in life. They embrace, not reject, industrial technology. To me, participatory education was just a distraction from the primary task of revolutionizing society.

I wanted a Red revolution. I had not joined the Communist Party; it was too tame, almost social democratic. Instead, I gravitated toward "PL": the partly Old Left, partly pro-Chinese Progressive Labor Movement, which was to become the Progressive Labor Party and years later would take over Students for a Democratic Society (SDS) and precipitate its demise.

Trendy Maoism was not what attracted me to PL; I was never convinced that Asiatic peasants had much to teach occidental workers. Instead, the Old Left virtues of PL appealed to me: its eagerness to establish links with the actual working class, its serene indifference to the egocentric impulses of students, and its disdain for adolescent urges to outrage the average American by flaunting bohemian attitudes toward sex, drugs, appearance, and work. In short, PL was tough and serious.

But to my astonishment, my fellow students were not moving in this direction. They were not interested in building a revolutionary workers' movement in America. They were instead moving on to the long-since-forgotten *Filthy* Speech Movement and then on to marijuana, LSD, "free universities" (where kinkiness and esoterica were

27

palmed off as radicalism), sexual experimentation, counterculture hair and clothing styles, and a new era in rock music. One Berkeley student captured the mood when he wrote that radicals "believe strongly that a movement that s----s together glues together...that Socialists who sleep together creep together."[8]

Student interest in social justice was essentially subordinate to interest in self-gratification and self-expression. I had assumed all along that American society was sick. But to discover *our* movement mirroring the sickness, instead of presenting a viable alternative, was a grievous letdown. The immoral drift of the upper reaches of society was not being resisted but rather accelerated by the movement. I agreed with Leslie Woolf Hedley who wrote at that time in a radical Old Left magazine that "bohemian decadence is not a force against the status quo, but a cancer caused by that status quo."[9]

In looking back with the benefit of some twenty years hindsight, I realize I should not be too harsh. Nowadays the campuses are quiet, as students— whose sexual morals show little improvement— busily prepare themselves for high-paying careers in the system, and preoccupy themselves with superficialities like fraternities and sororities, proper etiquette, and "dressing for success." The excessive self-centeredness here is plain for all to see. But in the early/mid 1960s, inordinate self-centeredness took different forms, and was camouflaged by a diffuse passion for social justice. However clouded their motives and twisted their personal morals, student radicals were at least *trying* to improve society and the world. They did reveal that at least they *cared*.

But when it comes to the arduous and complex matter of social justice, "caring" may not be sufficient. As the old adage has it, the road to hell is paved with good intentions, never mind partially good intentions.

As my fellow radicals were moving into decadence, or what would later be euphemistically called "personal liberation," they struck me as being rather messed-up, sufficiently disoriented so that they lacked the internal resources of courage and discipline to be able to change society for the better. How can you put someone else's house in order when your own languishes in chaos? This traditional bit of wisdom was nowhere to be heard in those days.

But the insight did come—slowly and with much pain—to some. In her autobiographical account of the Berkeley New Left scene of the 1960s, Sara Davidson mentioned one hapless fellow who announced that all of Berkeley was going crazy. His wife had left him, taking the children to join a gay collective. In a flash of perception, he exclaimed:

> In the last six months every knock on the door has been someone in anguish. Can you imagine the chutzpah? Trying to change the world when our personal lives are such a mess? Look at me. I'm twenty-nine years old and I'm living in a flophouse on Shattuck [Avenue] that has p--s-stained carpets and foul odors.[10]

The New Left, it seemed, could largely be understood in terms of subjective, personal imperatives. Students were too often using politics to act out problems that were essentially interior, be they metaphysical meaninglessness, alienation, neurosis, guilt, or whatever. "The result," noted Robert Brustein, a drama critic and puzzled radical, "is not revolution but rather theatre—a product of histrionic personalities and staged events."[11]

To me, the self-obsession of bourgeois students was a bourgeois phenomenon. The neo-Marxist historian Eugene Genovese was to make this point years later when he said that New Leftists "are the problem children of the solid bourgeoisie and constitute a problem for the Left only because their antics are confused with left-wing politics by the working class and lower middle class."[12]

I despaired.

T W O

OVER AND BACK

All political power in the German Democratic Republic [East Germany] is exercised by the working people. • *Article Two, Constitution of the German Democratic Republic*

In 1965, just before graduating from Berkeley, I married Elena Reyes. Although my best man was the brother of a leading figure in the Communist Party, my bride was neither a student nor an activist. She was, mercifully, uncomplicated and unaffected, and we married for the simple, nonideological reason of love.

Of mixed Filipino and Mexican-American parentage (her father, John, was a first-generation Filipino-American who worked in a defense factory and later as a barber), she intuitively identified with common people. Before our wedding our views had already coincided. She was no more infatuated with the New Left movement than I. Finding hope in neither our country nor its supposed antithesis, the movement, we decided to leave both country and movement.

We considered moving to Cuba, and we spent

our honeymoon in Mexico City so that we could visit the Cuban embassy. Since Elena was fluent in Spanish, Cuba was a natural choice. But we soon became suspicious of that option. Cuba was immensely popular with precisely those movement people we could not take seriously. Cuba was too glamorous, as was China.

We were ready to begin a new life in a new land. We wanted a society where we could settle down, raise a family, and participate somehow in humanity's steady march toward communism—a society that was militant, yet not an object of idolization by the New Left.

Why not East Germany? I thought. It was somewhat familiar since I had been there briefly. East Germany was quite militant, given its conflict situation with West Germany and the North Atlantic Treaty Organization (NATO). Moreover, it represented Communism's most advanced penetration into modern Western society and as such would be particularly interesting and congenial to Americans.

SETTING SAIL

Going to East Germany, or the German Democratic Republic (GDR) as it is officially called, is not like going to France or West Germany. One doesn't just show up and start doing whatever one wants. But since we didn't want to negotiate with East German officialdom from a distance, we thought the thing to do would be to travel to West Berlin, establish our base of operations there, and then negotiate directly with the officials.

I took a German language course. Then we put

ourselves and all our belongings on a bus destined for New York City, where we boarded a ship for Bremerhaven. From there we took a train directly to West Berlin. No side trips, no holidays. It was a direct shot, and a literal leap of faith.

On our first day in East Berlin we pounded on doors at this ministry and that. Since migration is usually from East to West, the East Berlin officials didn't know quite what to do with us. We were told that East Germany does not have foreign workers as West Germany has. Thus, it was impossible to move into a flat and take a job. On the other hand, East Germany doesn't welcome people who come and stay indefinitely while doing nothing at all. And since we weren't fugitives, we had to do *something*.

In our initial contacts we encountered a small colony of American fugitives living in East Berlin—American radicals who, because of McCarthyism, had fled *to* East Germany in the 1950s and enjoyed the great distinction of being known as victims of McCarthyism. One was a portly black political cartoonist whose work still appeared in black newspapers in the States. He lived in a bright new apartment with a beautiful blonde woman. He owned a Simca sedan, was able to take frequent trips to Paris, and seemed complacent about everything, from politics to his own situation.

Another black man made radio broadcasts aimed at black American GI's in Western Europe: lots of soul music and jive, with politics spliced in between. This lean cat, who had access to plenty of money and was proud of the turf he had marked off for himself, nevertheless had a curious air of missed opportunities about him and seemed constantly on the prowl.

Another such fugitive was the East Berlin correspondent for the *National Guardian,* a now-defunct pro-Soviet weekly paper in the States. She lived on the prestigious Karl-Marx-Allee in a very spacious and comfortable apartment, and she was married to an important functionary in the East German party.

Another fugitive—the most impressive of the lot—worked for the Paul Robeson Archive, where he put together materials on the life of Robeson, the noted black American singer and Communist. He was an informed and serious Marxist who nevertheless had a keen sense of the shortcomings of the East German government. Chastened but still committed, he had melancholy in his eyes, which evoked our respect and sympathy.

In our search to find a way to live in East Germany, we wound up at the Ministry for Higher Education. Since the East German Communists regarded the Free Speech Movement as, in their words, "a genuinely oppositional force" (unlike routine liberal causes in America), the officials at that ministry were particularly interested in us. After many visits there, it was agreed that we would become students. We were told that our application for study in East Germany would be forwarded to another ministry (never identified) and that the procedure would take quite some time. We were also told to continue living in West Berlin, get jobs there, and improve our German while our application was being processed.

It didn't occur to us at the time that we might present something of a security problem to the

East German government. We didn't realize that Berlin had long been a center for international intrigue. Every other week we were to enter East Berlin for a rendezvous with certain officials of the Socialist Unity Party, which is what the Communist party calls itself in East Germany. One official was from the Ministry for Higher Education and attached to the American-GDR Friendship Society. Another official was supposedly just the first man's friend but clearly acted as his superior. We never learned what he represented.

The ostensible purpose of these meetings was to show us the sights of East Berlin. The actual purpose, which in our innocence we did not suspect, was to find out if we were for real. Later, other East Germans told us that our interracial marriage probably did more than anything else to reassure the security officials, since in their minds such a marriage would be anathema to CIA operatives.

We wound up waiting five-and-a-half months in West Berlin. After an arduous search, we had found a single room in Kreuzberg (then a working-class district of West Berlin): no bath, no shower, no hot water, no refrigerator, no phone, no washing machine or dryer. But the room *did* have a view—of a parking lot enclosed by four walls. In addition, we faced freezing, bitter cold weather throughout most of our stay. Our heat came from a dirty old coal furnace, which we never effectively learned to operate. With a fifty-and-one-half-hour work week, we usually left for our jobs before sunup and returned after sundown. It was a taste of real poverty, and no doubt a test of our resolve to enter the East.

Oddly enough, our jobs were at the British military base. There we learned firsthand of the British laxness in security matters, not the least of which was the incredible fact that we were assigned to the BRIXMIS unit (British Commanders-in-Chief Mission to the Soviet Forces in Germany). This outfit handled liaison with the Soviet military in East Berlin. It sent British personnel into East Berlin by car on a daily basis in order to reaffirm Allied rights in the Soviet zone, and it was also involved in espionage.

I witnessed the installation of special flashlights in BRIXMIS cars, which enabled the British to read maps without being spotted by the Vopo (East German police) while they engaged in various reconnaissance activities under the cover of darkness. I worked in the auto depot, where cars would frequently return with smashed headlights, banged fenders, and broken axles resulting from high-speed chases through the back streets of East Berlin. Several mechanics were employed full-time to repair these cars.

My job was to wash cars, sweep garages, lift heavy things for the sergeant, crack ice banks and frozen roads with a pick, shovel ice and snow off the roads, and clean latrines. Elena worked in the BRIXMIS kitchen, scrubbing floors on her hands and knees, cutting vegetables, doing dishes, and also washing latrines. Sometimes I was able to sneak over to the kitchen to see her, and—if the alcoholic German chef was in a good mood—warm my insides with some hot tea or soup.

LIVING IN THE EAST, TEMPORARILY

We finally learned that we would be admitted to East Berlin, but only for four-and-a-half months. Our East German visas would not allow us to travel back and forth at will to West Berlin, although one of us would be allowed to make one trip. (We did not realize then that that was a programmed way of holding a hostage.) We were given insert visas, that is, visas that could be removed from our passports once we left (so, we were told later, there would be no evidence we had ever been in East Germany).

Before we were admitted we were instructed that "the struggle" was back in the United States and we would eventually have to return there. It was hard to argue with seasoned Communists on that score. Besides, we were absolutely delighted with the privilege of a new, albeit temporary, life in what we believed was a workers' state.

We thought the prospect of living in East Berlin represented a rare—and dangerous, to be sure—opportunity since there were then no diplomatic relations between East Germany and the United States. As for danger, however, given the escalating Vietnam War and the draft, we actually felt safer in East Germany than in the United States.

Many years later the FBI told us that the probable reason we had been treated to an all-expenses-paid stay in East Germany was because the security service thought we could be useful agents for them back in the States. Furthermore, there had apparently been some competition for us; the FBI indicated that one of our regular East German friends was probably a Soviet agent. But while we were there, we were totally oblivious to all these machinations.

So, after five-and-a-half months of existence in West Berlin, we packed up all our goods and hired two spacious taxis to take our little household to Checkpoint Charlie, one way. The taxi drivers were mystified but asked no questions.

Once we arrived, the East German customs official had to go through all our suitcases and trunks. Before long he came to our collection of books, many of them about the Soviet Union and Marxism but written by non-Marxists. He told us we could not take them in because they were "antidemocratic." Now, *we* were mystified.

I became angry and began shouting at the official. He yelled back, officiously. Soon, my wife began crying. The official blushed, hunkered back, and finally disappeared. We were holding our ground.

A while later he reappeared. He told us the trunks containing books would have to be tied up with wire and fastened with offical lead seals that could be broken only by another, more senior, customs official in an office across town. If we broke the seals ourselves, we would be in serious trouble.

Our ordeal at Checkpoint Charlie took hours. When we were finally permitted into the East, night had fallen. East Berlin closes down early in the evening, so we had trouble finding taxis. When we did locate some, the drivers refused to take us and our load because our things were too heavy for their precious (and brittle?) cars. We were furious. We took all our things to the nearest intersection, piled them up, and sat on them. More hours passed—and then it began to rain. We were tempted to go back to the West.

Little did we realize that our impromptu sit-down strike had embarrassed the East German customs officials at Checkpoint Charlie; they had been keeping a nervous eye on us all the while. Finally, just after Elena and I agreed to camp out there for the entire night and call our Party contacts the next morning, a customs official jogged out to us and announced that an army truck was on its way to pick us up and transport our encampment to our prearranged guest quarters in the Pankow district of East Berlin. We were amazed that something was finally going to happen.

Within minutes a huge army truck rumbled up to our little kingdom, and seven or eight burly soldiers poured out the back. They swept our belongings and us into the back of the truck, and soon we were bumping along on our way to Pankow. When we arrived at our new address near midnight, the man in charge got out of the front of the truck, rang the doorbell, and banged furiously on the door, yelling "Polizei! Polizei!" ("Police! Police!").

The hostess was roused from her sleep and came running down the stairs from the third floor. The door opened, the shaken hostess was given instructions, and before we knew it the soldiers had the suitcases and heavy trunks on their shoulders and were marching double-time up the stairs to the third floor. The hostess meanwhile prepared our bedding and linens, and she was kind enough to ignite the difficult coal furnace for us. We offered tips to the soldiers and hostess but were refused. Before long, we were in bed, fast asleep, dreaming of the next day when we would see about getting those seals off our trunks. We did manage to do that after complaining to the right people.

The official reason we were admitted to East Berlin was to be students at the philosophy department at Humboldt University (formerly the University of Berlin). It turned out not to be the usual student life.

For one thing, we entered during the middle of the term, hardly the way to go about studying philosophy. Then when we went to the university for our first class, the classroom was empty. Classes had been canceled because all the male students were on military maneuvers. Classes didn't begin again until about three weeks later. That left only a month or so of classes before summer vacation.

We were visited each week by a Party official— but not for the purpose of discussing the finer points of philosophy. Of course, we didn't bother ourselves with the possibility that studying philosophy might not have been the real reason we had been admitted to the East.

NO NEW MAN

We had thought we would find a new kind of human being in East Germany. We had believed that in a society based on private ownership of the means of production, most people could not help being materialistic and hedonistic. But we expected that in a society based on the collective ownership of the means of production and the inculcation of communist morality, people would become noticeably selfless and courageous.

What we actually discovered was that the human beings in the East were fundamentally no different—no better, no worse—than those of West Berlin or the United States. East Berliners, Communists or not, young or old, were no less interested in themselves, their incomes, possessions, vacations, personal luxuries, and careers than people in the West. I must stress that the Party members were by no means the evil ogres some Americans love to fantasize and fret about. No, not that. But they weren't inspiring figures either.

One young Communist functionary in his twenties worked for the Afro-Asian Solidarity Committee and was so important that he enjoyed his own chauffeured limousine and private secretaries. He was simply ecstatic about a Danish ball-point pen he had brought back from a recent trip to Budapest. On the outside of the pen was the picture of a girl, who appeared nude when the pen was turned upside down. That ball-point pen seemed to ignite far more enthusiasm in him than the questions of Vietnam, a burning issue at the time, or of Afro-Asian solidarity. Was he the new Communist man?

We were introduced by the alleged Soviet agent, a kindly family man, to a man who represented East German exports in Holland, Belgium, and Great Britain. He described himself as *parteilich parteilos*, meaning Party-minded though not technically a Party member. A man in his thirties, he sported a Western suit, blue turtleneck sweater with matching socks, Pall Mall cigarettes (never before seen by us in East Germany), and a Paper Mate pen.

He drove a tiny Russian-made Moskovitch. He said that if he saved enough money he would like to buy a better car. What would it be? we asked. An

East German Wartburg? A French Simca? A Czech-made Tatra? No. It was going to be a Jaguar Mark IX limousine! Could this man actually be a Jaguar communist? Apparently so. What, we puzzled, would cause a Party-minded man to be interested in such things? Status seeking? An addiction to material things? Corruption by the West? We didn't ask, but we were bowled over. We feared that this man symbolized the future of East German society.

This consumerist mentality was an impending moral problem for East Germany, but only a few East Germans were aware of it—one a Catholic, one the American fugitive who worked at the Paul Robeson Archive, and one a simple humanitarian lady who was fond of quoting Elena's dictum ("affluence breeds decadence") to her friends.

We had been looking for a new quality of life. But for East Germans, Communism basically meant more possessions, a new *quantity* in life—specifically, the promise of a standard of living even higher than that of West Germany. That might be a laudable goal, but we hardly thought it constituted the essence of Communism. After all, if Communism was simply about abundance, countries such as the United States or West Germany obviously had little need of it.

Before the Berlin Wall went up, West Germany had lured millions of East Germans westward by means of higher wages and living standards, helped along by the Marshall Plan and other initial advantages. One could understand the East German government's desire to neutralize this appeal by outstripping West Germany in standard of living and by fanning the flames of consumerism in the East (in 1974, East Germany would overtake Great Britain in per capita income). In a sense, one could blame the West for infecting the East with the consumerist virus. But on the other hand, Marxism is a materialistic philosophy, and precious little in it can innoculate anyone against consumerist materialism.

We complained to Party members that the people of East Germany seemed just as avaricious as those living under capitalism. They explained to us that "nothing is too good for the worker." Yes, but...We suggested they were eventually going to turn the heroic worker into an effete idler. They, in turn, accused us of seeking to promote a *Proletkult*—something that had been tried and discarded in the Soviet Union, always the court of highest appeal.

We asserted that workers should be able to enter the finest restaurants in their work clothes instead of the required coat and tie. We were Proletkultists, they said. We thought it un-socialist for some celebrities and professionals to get paid so much money that after having bought a country villa, two cars, vacations to Paris, and prized caseloads of American whiskey they still had more money at their disposal than they could think how to spend. Again, we were declared Proletkultists.

In short, we had expected Communism to be an affirmation of working-class culture. I don't think we were opposed to the improvement of the material conditions of the working class. What we dreaded was a working class that coveted the possessions and jaded lifestyle of the uncharitable and undisciplined rich.

We wanted the working class to struggle against

bourgeois idols, not bow down before them. We didn't want the next generation of East German youth to look like the kids at Berkeley—spoiled, confused, alienated, questing after excitement and lost meaning.

We thought that, in a society where workers hold all political power, the spirit of solidarity, sacrifice, and simplicity (which has historically infused working-class organizations, such as trade unions) would permeate society as a whole. But the only difference between East and West seemed to be that while the people on both sides were materialistic, those in the West were more selfish in a dog-eat-dog way. In the West the emphasis is more on affluence for *oneself;* in the East the emphasis is somewhat more on affluence for *everyone.* This distinction might be a significant moral and practical one, but it did not reassure or inspire us.

Most people who abandon Communism will agree that a communist society is a magnificent ideal. That was not quite our feeling. The ultimate goal of communism seemed to be simply to universalize Beverly Hills, Grosse Pointe, and Scarsdale. What was depressing was the apparent desire to make everybody rich. Increased wealth for all, as such, did not seem a goal worth dedicating our lives to.

The problem did not seem to us to be characteristic of East Germany alone but of Communism as a whole. Sure, we reasoned, a great proportion of the people of China and Cuba might be—or seem to be—selfless and heroic. But a generation or two hence, when affluence is achieved, would the same ethos prevail? We doubted it.

In quitting Communism we did not become mili-

tant anti-Communists. We just became rather indifferent to Communism. It was perhaps unfair of
us to expect a strikingly new quality to life in East
Germany. After all, the new order was a mere six-
teen years old at the time and had tremendous economic and sociopsychological obstacles to
overcome. Nevertheless, neither the direction East
German society was taking nor the East German
"man of the future" engendered confidence.

Moreover, we became increasingly aware that
the workers did not actually hold political power,
as was claimed. The Party bureaucracy did. Although we still thought that a socialized economy—but one where the workers, not the
bureaucracy, ran things—could help people become more considerate of each other, we believed
that a socialized economy by itself was insuffi-
cient to dramatically improve human relations.
Our experiences in the East, neither wholly positive nor wholly negative, took the messianic zeal
out of our interest in socialism of any kind. It was
dawning on us that there were more important
things in life than only politics and ideology. The
old polarities and absolutes were melting away.

And yet, my fundamental sense of solidarity
with the "man with the hoe," the common man,
never has melted away. Although many individual
Marxists have no authentic interest in or rapport
with actual common people, Marxism nonetheless
teaches that any decent political movement that
finds no room for the working class is a fraud.

Eugene Genovese, the neo-Marxist, put the matter crisply: "If we can't win these people, we're not
going to win anything worth winning."[1] In this
sense, I must respect the original Marxist inten-

tion, however much betrayed in practice, of bringing dignity, justice, and sovereignty to the working class. But I am no longer in any sense a Marxist, and I think it is fortunate that there are other ways of expressing solidarity with working people.

Returning to the States in 1966, we observed that the New Left had gotten bigger, more radical, and more comprehensive in its critique of American society. At Berkeley, where I returned to get my doctorate and Elena finished her undergraduate work, we maintained a strict aloofness from the movement. It was a lonely position to be in, and a curious one, since one reason for our aloofness was our continued identification with the working class.

The movement had learned nothing about the worker and his way of life. In fact, the working class was dismissed as a political point of reference and was often held in open contempt.

To be sure, the movement was able to sympathize with certain lower orders: Vietnamese peasants, American Indians on Alcatraz, welfare recipients, convicted criminals. But the movement did not divide society into elites and masses, but rather, as Tom Wolfe hinted,[2] into the hip and funky on the one hand and the drab and dreary on the other. Or, as Sara Davidson, a Berkeley sorority radical, put it: "We divided people into two groups: those who knew, and those who didn't know. Aldous Huxley and Carson McCullers knew. Roy Rogers and Doris Day didn't."[3]

Thus, the issue of economic class was niftily sidestepped. To people with this world view Vietnamese peasants *and* students at Ivy League universities, welfare recipients *and* with-it philanthropists, convicted criminals *and* opulent entertainers all stood shoulder to shoulder on the same side of the Great Chasm: they were all funky. On the other side stood the mass of tacky know-nothings.

We realized that the foe of the working class was not merely the corporate elite but also the New Left, the radical but pseudopopulist students and intellectuals. Instinctively, we understood why average people could be heard complaining that the educated had become vain, pompous, and swollen with self-importance.

All in all, the New Left was hardly a populistic movement, whether in the sense of being a movement of common people or in the sense of being a movement whose priorities were geared to the regular working class. In the years during and after the FSM, the radicals had generally squandered their chance of becoming a movement for the people.

AN OUTPOST OF
GOD'S KINGDOM

When we look at the churches in the eastern parts of Europe we can see something of the truth of Christ's word, "the last shall be first." • *Martin Niemoeller*

Entangled with the story told so far is another drama, which requires a separate telling. This one pertains to the fact that in East Berlin I was converted to Christianity, or perhaps I should say I returned to Christ after a period of absence.

I was born and raised for a time in the Dutch-ethnic Christian Reformed Church but did most of my growing up in the enormous and evangelical Hollywood Presbyterian Church. Hollywood Presbyterian was a church "on fire" for God, but somehow it didn't fully warm my soul.

A CHRISTIAN ISSUE

In 1956, my fellow Sunday schoolers were bedecked with "I Like Ike" buttons. Dad and I liked Stevenson, though our first choice had been populist Estes Kefauver. Was this a small matter? Not to the son and grandson of immigrants imbued with a respect for the common man and persuaded that the Democratic Party was on his side.

But if it wasn't a small matter, was it a Christian matter? Even at the tender age of twelve, I had somehow noticed that wealth and the gospel are in historic tension. This observation, of course, wasn't original. Others who had read the Bible before me saw the same thing.

One of the most poignant passages in Scripture for me was where Jesus warns the outwardly righteous that they stand in danger of the Judgment. To them, Jesus will say when He comes in glory at the end of the world: "Depart from me, ye cursed, into everlasting fire." Why? "For I was hungered, and ye gave me no meat: I was thirsty, and ye gave me no drink....Verily I say unto you, inasmuch as ye did it not to one of the least of these [my brethren], ye did it not to me" (Matt. 25:41–45).

Then, I surmised, Christ will often come to us in the guise of the least advantaged of people. To want to aid them is to want to aid Jesus. My reasoning took another step: to vote Republican was to lean toward the rich and away from the least advantaged. So my reasoning led me to believe that the coming election was indeed a Christian matter.

Things at church became further complicated for me two years later. My Sunday school colleagues went to Hollywood High, a partying school, but I did not live in the Hollywood area, so I went to Dorsey, a "bad" school in central Los Angeles. How bad? Well, one year our champion pole vaulter was arrested and sent to jail on murder charges. A white bully intentionally cracked open a black guy's skull with a baseball bat during P.E. class. A friend, who later would be an usher in our wedding, threw a pipe bomb into a school bus one afternoon, injuring several kids. Then, after a football game with Manual Arts High, a white guy sitting idly in a car adjacent to our campus was knifed by a black dude from Manual. Later that year, after a game at Fremont High, some Fremont fans picked up a section of the bleachers and pushed it over the side of the stadium onto a group of Dorsey pupils passing by below. Heroin was available at the little market across from our campus.

Dorsey was racially mixed but internally (and unofficially) segregated. Racial tensions were high, and riots broke out occasionally, once causing a local TV station to do a special on "the problem" at Dorsey. Given my straightforward desire to obey Christ and follow Scripture, I knew that to despise "the least of these" was not allowed me. So, I threw myself into the fledgling integrationist efforts at Dorsey.

But at church my fellow Bible-believing Sunday school chums—plus the teachers and ministers— seemed utterly oblivious to the plight of the least of our brethren. To be sure, Hollywood is not central L.A., but I sensed that the things agitating my soul were not peculiar to me. It was the late 1950s and very early 1960s, after all. The civil rights movement—led and supported by many Christian people, black and white—was gathering national momentum. A justice issue was facing all American Christians, but the Hollywood evangelicals— absorbed in beach parties and weenie roasts and hymn sings—did not pay attention.

THE SHIFT

After high school, I entered UCLA and eventually met some Episcopalians who were discussing the need for improved race relations, world peace, and socialized medicine. This was the extra dimension in Christianity I was looking for but could not find in evangelicalism.

After two years at UCLA, I transferred to Berkeley in search of greater sociopolitical involvement and was there confirmed an Episcopalian by the late Bishop James A. Pike.

My membership in the Episcopal Church quickly got me—unintentionally—tangled in the web of modernist theology. My hero of the moment, Bishop Pike, was not only speaking up for social justice but also publicly jettisoning central Christian doctrines such as the Incarnation, the Trinity, and the physical Resurrection of Jesus Christ.

Pike was not an original thinker, but he did have a way of capturing one's imagination. He, and others like him, led me to read Paul Tillich and Rudolf Bultmann. I noticed that for some reason, the social action emphasis went hand in hand with doctrinal skepticism. Although I didn't particularly want to surrender my belief in a supernatural God, miracles, an afterlife, and all the rest, that seemed to be the thing to do if one wanted to be a political radical. That one could combine theological orthodoxy with working for political and economic justice didn't seem to be an option. I knew of no compelling role models among either evangelicals or Episcopalians for orthodox social action.

My political views soon became Marxist, however, thus posing the issue of faith and politics at a different level. But to my comfort, I knew that I could easily reconcile Christianity with Marxism, provided my theology was modernistic. So, modernism it would be.

Soon after Elena and I arrived in West Berlin, the *New York Times* carried stories about a new Death-of-God theology surfacing in the States. Just reading about it brought to a head the question of whether I was still a Christian at all.

ATHEISM IN DISGUISE

Modernism is a very slippery slope. Once you begin reinterpreting, rationalizing, and demythologizing the faith, no objective criterion exists by which you can distinguish what in Christianity is mythic or symbolic from what is actually true. The only criterion is subjective—what you as the self-appointed spokesperson for modern man find palatable and believable. Whatever fails to pass your private tests, from the Virgin Birth to the deity of Christ, can be considered mythic and reinterpreted in secular terms. This approach is a very convenient one.

Once you have hacked away at those doctrines, nothing prevents your being consistently modern and demythologizing God Himself. The Death-of-God theologians, by being consistent and thoroughly honest about their procedures, did exactly that. They continued to esteem the *man* Jesus and thus called themselves "Christian atheists," but they were regular atheists in every sense of the word.

The more I reflected, the more I recognized that the theological modernism I had imbibed was in fact a shrouded atheism. Modernism's assumptions were atheistic: man need only believe what he finds believable, and nothing miraculous or paradoxical is included. The logical conclusion of modernism is atheism. In my heart I knew I didn't believe in Jesus Christ in any significant sense, nor did I have a relationship with Him. I wanted to continue calling myself a Christian, but I didn't want to fool myself. The fact was that Christ made no difference in my life. I decided that the Death-of-God theologians were fearless men, and honesty demanded that I face the cold truth that I, too, was an atheist. Not a Christian atheist, mind you, but a Marxist atheist. (Elena's faith was firmer, and she never quite gave in to atheism, even though she too embraced Marxism.)

When we moved into East Berlin, I was still looking for a "new man," only now he would have to be the new *communist* man, a man willing and able to transcend self-interest. I didn't find him.

Much to my surprise, the Christians in East Berlin were the ones transcending self-interest. They had to pay a price to practice their faith. Although they weren't physically tortured or martyred, they—especially the youth—were subject to constant challenge, ridicule, harassment, and discrimination. Their faith was always being tested.

Now, be clear on this point: we don't like the political and cultural props knocked out from under our faith. We don't like to have to stand on the promises of the Lord. None of us likes to have our faith put to the test—I know I certainly don't. It hurts. But as the maxim says, "no pains, no gains," which is nowhere more true than in the life of the faith.

In East Germany, the doubters, minimizers, reductionists, and demythologizers are ill-suited for survival. Theologies constructed upon doubt, moral laxity, or compromise with atheism simply do not stand up to constant badgering and intimidation. Hence, the theological tone of the East German church is rigorous. As the American Lutheran theologian John Warwick Montgomery, a frequent traveler to East Germany, noted: "The theology from the pulpit is almost always orthodox and biblical...theological liberalism is a luxury that no church in crisis, with its back to the wall, can afford."[1]

A MAN OF GOD

Soon after arriving in East Berlin we met a Protestant pastor who made a profound impression on us. In Berlin during the Second World War, he had once been a student of the Protestant theologian Dietrich Bonhoeffer, who was killed by the Nazis in 1945. Also, the pastor had been a member of the Confessing Church, the Protestant minority that resisted Hitler. He had even spent a short time in a Nazi prison.

I decided to ask this pastor about his call to the ministry. What does he—a traditional German male and very much the patriarch of his family—do? I was totally unprepared for his reaction, because he cried. This man had seemingly been touched by God at the core of his being. What he told us about his call and his walk with the Lord was amazing—and thoroughly believable.

For example, he said the Holy Spirit would sometimes take control of his heart in the pulpit and override his prepared sermon. He would become a vehicle through whom the Word of God was revealed and proclaimed. His statements were not intended to be figurative, glib, or melodramatic. For once, and only once, he was visited by the Spirit so profoundly that he spoke in tongues while he was preaching in the pulpit.

This pastor, by the way, said nothing about being a charismatic or a neo-Pentecostalist. Remember, it was 1966. It was unlikely the neo-Pentecostalist movement, which was to blossom in the States a year later, had yet reached East Berlin.

I learned about all this *after* Easter Sunday 1966, which is an important date for me. On that Sunday I was converted to Christ as a result of hearing that pastor's sermon proclaiming the physical Resurrection of Jesus Christ.

I still find it odd that as a new and enthused Marxist I would be converted by a single sermon, in a foreign language I was still learning, in a drab little Protestant church inside a Communist mecca. But so it was. An invisible transcendent power was in the pastor's message: it caused the scales to fall from my eyes. I could hardly doubt what he told us about the way the Holy Spirit empowered his ministry, because something extraordinary coming from that pulpit had hit *me*.

Other, more subtle, factors were surely at work in that church too. As I noted in my diary: "There is a mysterious and very vibrant quality about church life here. The worshipers are most fervent, yet reverent, and their quiet enthusiasm spills over and fills the whole congregation."

The inside of that church was dreary: the pews were gray; the walls were cracked and peeling. There were no majestic choirs or fancy vestments or "amens" shouted from the congregation, or impressive statuary...or anything one could call fetching or attention-grabbing. The setting was "all wrong." And yet—it wasn't.

What we had very unexpectedly bumped into in East Berlin was the primitive church, the "church of the poor." What happened to me was caused by more than one man, for I could see Jesus in the church of the poor and despised, whereas I really couldn't find Him in the church of the prosperous and respected. In the States I had found Christianity a feeble thing. As part of the social establishment, it was respectable and insipid. And those churches which weren't quite respectable seemed hell-bent on becoming so.

Yes, I had heard the gospel back in the States, but perhaps the American ecclesiastical context had blunted its impact on me. In East Berlin, I heard the gospel in a different language and in a different context, and it commanded my attention and whole-hearted response.

THE GIVERS

One of the best friends we had in East Berlin was a Roman Catholic who taught Greek and Latin in a Catholic school. He told us he would never have a chance to study for his doctorate, because the state doesn't need Ph.D.'s in Greek and Latin. Furthermore, non-Party people such as himself had a hard time getting permission to study for a doctorate in the humanities.

Although he did express hope that Communism would become more tolerant, he never indicated any personal resentment about the disadvantage he suffered as a Catholic Christian. Indeed, he stressed that the Roman Catholic Church was exceptionally healthy in East Germany. He noted that the Church no longer had as much property as it once had, certainly not the kind of holdings and businesses Catholics have in West Germany. However, he said, the Catholic parishes in East Germany are full—and full of sincere believers.

When I asked him to explain why he thought that was true, he emphasized that people in East Germany can *get* nothing from church; they can only *give*. He commented that there were no more careerists and hangers-on as were plentiful in West Germany. (Interestingly, in a 1963 letter to an East German pastor, the eminent Protestant theologian Karl Barth noted that because of their "sheer security," the churches in West Germany "are under the threat of spiritual indolence.")[2]

Our Catholic friend went on to speak distastefully of how West German politicians, especially ones in the Christian political party called the Christian Democratic Union, must show themselves in church on Sundays in order to get ahead in politics. Too often such people, and the middle classes generally, identified themselves as Christians only for what they could get out of church: respectability, prestige, acceptable social life, and business contacts.

In contrast, the East German careerists and climbers flocked around the Party, not around the churches. Too bad for the Party, but good for the churches!

In East Germany, people who remain in the churches become more intense Christians in that they must rely more directly on the working of the Holy Spirit in their lives. Being a sincere believer cuts one off from having influence in society, from having connections of the useful sort, and it often means a meager wage, lack of preferment for education, jobs, and housing. The Christian there finds himself saying, literally, with the psalmist: "God is my helper, the Lord the mainstay of my life" (Ps. 54:4 NEB). Church attendance is not a ritualized or perfunctory thing; it is not the frosting on an already abundant life. No, the abundant life, in the sense Christ promised it, is discovered in the midst of deprivation.

TO SERVE,
NOT TO RULE

The Christian in the East...can no longer live on the illusion of his respectability.... He is completely thrown back on Christ. • *Helmut Gollwitzer*

One day Elena and I were walking along East Berlin's well-known Friedrichstrasse. Just as we were about to cross a street, a black sedan crossed in front of us with a man inside who looked just like D. Moritz Mitzenheim, the Protestant bishop of the Thuringian region. We ran after the car and followed it around a corner to a spot in front of a hospice where it parked.

After a second look inside the car, we were positive it was he. We decided to throw caution to the winds and say hello to him. We introduced ourselves as Americans interested in the situation of the churches in East Germany and exchanged a few pleasantries with the bishop. Then, for fear of being too imposing, we said thank you and goodby, and we walked away.

Before we got far away, the driver of the car got out and yelled to us, indicating the bishop wanted to speak to us further. When we got back to the car, the bishop, who was then seventy-five years old, got out, shook hands with us, and invited us to go into the hospice with him. We were thrilled.

The bishop had come to the hospice to pick up an assistant. While we waited he asked us about our activities. Then he told us about the two times he had visited America. This turned our talk to politics. "There is no such thing as a 'Christian government' or an 'atheist government,' " he commented. "Governments are simply governments."

Then he made an incisive remark: "Christians in the GDR are called to *serve* and *not to rule.*" His statement resonates wonderfully with the teachings found in the pages of the New Testament, but it is quite different from the declarations of Latin American liberation theologians and certain Christians in the United States who urge Christians to charge into politics in the name of Jesus and take power.

We were impressed by the serene warmth of Bishop Mitzenheim, who had been a prominent leader of the anti-Nazi Confessing Church during the Hitler era. He had spoken softly but emphatically during our brief meeting.

The East German churches have a problem with the never-say-die reactionaries who are nostalgic for times when Christians did indeed rule, when church and government were locked in a compromising embrace. There is an analogous problem with pro-Communist church members who would make the servant church into a *subservient* church. The regime readily utilizes these people and rewards them according to their usefulness in getting the churches to be mouthpieces for state policies. Although some of these people have high visibility, they are not trusted inside the churches and usually have very little influence there. Some may have honorable motives, but they enjoy privileges while the great majority of Christians suffer discrimination and abuse. This fact denies them credibility inside the very churches they try to speak for.

Most of these people are *not* members of the ruling Socialist Unity Party in East Germany and cannot be considered outright Communists. Unlike most other Communist countries, East Germany allows Christians to join the Party, though the Party reserves the right to "educate" such recalcitrants in atheism and "recommend" that they resign their church membership. In practice, a Party member who is a churchgoer is a rarity—and getting rarer.

Everyone we knew agreed that one would never find an enthusiastic Party member who is also an enthusiastic churchgoer. Because the inner tensions would be so great, such a person would be ardent about one but perfunctory about the other. Marxism-Leninism is officially atheistic and philosophically materialist. Riddled with Gnostic and Pelagian assumptions, it is totalistic in its claims on the heart and mind. I believe it is impossible to blend orthodox Christianity with Marxism or for Christians to give complete allegiance to *any* civil government, even though in the West, most Christians resolutely identify themselves with national ideologies and ambitions.

Consequently and ironically, because Marxism-Leninism by its opposition can purify Christianity, it can be *functionally* pro-Christian, contrary to its own intentions. Because of Communism's rigid and sometimes punitive separation of church and state, few orthodox Christians are tempted to, or find themselves in any way able to, identify their faith with the Communist state. Thus, while Communists are willing to use a few willing Christians in certain instances, the "throne-and-altar" disease (or, in the United States, the "God-and-country" virus) is much less likely to take hold in a Communist society than in just about any other kind.

The foes of the Christian faith who are in government and the upper echelons of society are more likely to openly advertise themselves as such in the East than in the West. Hence, the idolization of the nation and the corruption and seduction of the churches by political ideology and national aspirations are much more vexing problems for Christians in the West than for those in the East.

What did I learn about Christianity from our sojourn in East Germany? Three things, none by itself unique but in combination all too rare. (1) *Theological modernism is a journey away from Christ, not toward Him.* This was certainly the case with me, and I've never seen any evidence that it has been otherwise with others. (2) As important as it is to transform social structures on behalf of the less fortunate, *to reduce Christianity to social reform alone is to sap it of its unique power*, the power to change lives, without which social reform is a superficial undertaking. (3) *One of the most insidious threats to the church today is our own militant anti-Communism.*

Of these three lessons, the first two I take to be virtually self-evident among most believers today.

But the third lesson—the danger of militant anti-Communism—is the point that must be stressed, from a solidly Christian point of view.

THE REAL FEAR

The extreme fear of Communism evident in so many American Christians results, I believe, from the *un*willingness to be tested by persecution. Here's the logic: Communists oppress the church and persecute Christians; therefore, Christians must see to it that America stands up to and one day banishes this demonic threat. The way to accomplish this is for true Christians to get into positions of power and influence and to rule.

We all (me included) want the good life; the last thing we welcome is suffering. Never mind that in the early church the greatest privilege was to be able to suffer and even be martyred like one's Lord and for one's Lord, since Christians are "heirs of God and fellow heirs with Christ, if indeed we suffer with Him in order that we may also be glorified with Him" (Rom. 8:17 NASB). Never mind that the East German Protestant pastor Johannes Hamel said that "when I suffer, I am bound to the Lord in his suffering."[1]

Never mind that Mother Teresa teaches that pain is the "kiss of Jesus" and that suffering is an occasion to rejoice because, for the Christian, suffering is "a sign that you have come so close to Him on the cross that He can kiss you."[2] Never mind that St. John of the Cross said that "when the soul is making most progress, it is travelling in darkness, knowing naught. Wherefore, since God

...is the Master and Guide of this blind soul, it may well and truly rejoice...and say: 'In darkness and secure.' "[3]

Today we seek to avoid the slightest suffering, don't we? Yet the saints throughout the ages have known and seen suffering not as a burden but as a gift and a joy. This does not mean we should revert to a kind of spiritual masochism, or an inordinate preoccupation with suffering, but we should be *willing* to suffer and not be preoccupied with our comfort and ease.

When Pope John Paul II was shot and almost killed, he promptly forgave his assailant in his heart and thanked God for allowing him to "experiment with pain." Later, he visited the man in prison and forgave him. How bizarre his behavior appears to most American believers! We say a loud no thanks to pain, for we would rather lay up more and more treasure on earth for ourselves and have our government protect it with nuclear bombs and missiles aimed at others who need Christ too.

What East Germany can show us is that the church can be most unmistakably the church when she is poor and thrown back on radical reliance on her Lord. But rather than relying on the Lord, rather than opening ourselves to a word from Him, rather than allowing Him to capture our tongues and speak, we would rather send our TV preachers to the White House to whisper sweet nothings into the ear of the president.

Don't get me wrong. I'm not recommending that the United States surrender to the Soviet Union, and I'm not urging Christians to seek out martyrdom. I haven't sold all my worldly goods and given the proceeds to the poor. I am no hero, either. But I am looking for a little more balance between self-interest and stepping forward in bolder faith. I am not prepared to take a self-inflicted one-way trip into the "dark night of the soul," but I am looking for a little more sensitivity to the ways of the Lord.

With Jesus Christ things are often not what they seem. Weakness is strength. Crucifixion issues forth in Resurrection.

THE STUFF OF SAINTS

In 1945, Russia began the sovietization of Poland. The West wept. But in 1978 the relatively unknown Karol Wojtyla emerged from Krakow, and the magnificent Pope John Paul II burst forth onto the world scene like a comet out of nowhere. The timing was so stunning that even many of our most ardent Protestants noted what appeared to be a work of the Holy Spirit.

If Karol Wojtyla had hailed from Tübingen or Utrecht or Paris (where modernism and moral laxity are rampant) instead of Krakow (where neither Communist nor Christian is interested in modernism or moral laxity), he would not likely have been the same steeled and unintimidated man of faith we see today. We must honestly ask how much stronger he would have been had he come from Grand Rapids, Wheaton, or Orange County—or New York, South Bend, or New Orleans.

In this situation, we would be foolish to equate, as the vast majority of modern, Bible-believing Christians do, the cause of Jesus Christ with the cause of the West. The Lord doesn't need the industrious West to work out His purposes. He doesn't need you or me. Conversely, He can use

Communists to accomplish His aims!

It is so typical of Jesus to provide for us in mysterious and totally unexpected ways, just as He did for the early church. But we Christians would rather save our own lives than step forward in dependence on our Lord and risk losing them. We really don't want to find our refuge in Him; we would prefer a nuclear umbrella.

Christian tradition insists that the amount of destruction one is willing to use in warfare be proportionate to the justice of one's cause, that innocent and defenseless noncombatants not be killed intentionally. Yet we instinctively turn a blind eye to the inherently indiscriminate killing wrought by nuclear weapons. Thus, most of us would rather risk inflicting incalculable destruction on both combatants and noncombatants among the world's peoples than allow our nation to take some chances for the sake of peace. Though we may claim we are resting on Christ's sufficiency and that we're heavenbound, we will not run the risk of suffering disadvantage or injustice to ourselves. Is what we are doing reflected in the ways of the saints in other times?

Of course, our attitudes make sense if power politics and national pride are ends in themselves. But somehow, it just doesn't seem that "America first" is the posture Jesus Himself would adopt; thus we must at least wonder if He would want us to adopt it. One thing is certain: "Caesar first" was not a part of His gospel arsenal.

EXCEPTIONAL BLESSINGS

Fine, you say, but you're talking about Poland

and East Germany, which are benign crucibles of faith compared to other places. Indeed. But there are no limits to God's faithfulness. Dmitri Dudko, a persecuted Orthodox priest in the Soviet Union, asked himself if as a result of Communism, faith is weaker in the East than in the West. He wrote, "On which soil is faith stronger? On the soil of sufferings, of the Cross. Faith withers on earthly well-being, and in the West there's well-being, so faith is weaker there."[4] This verdict echoes the venerable words of Tertullian from the early church: "The blood of the martyrs is the seed of the church."

But we pragmatic Americans don't have time for such "mysticism." We're smart. We live in the real world, and we think we know how grace can be successfully repressed. We instinctively fret that God might let the faith become obsolete if we don't do something to repel the bad guys, forgetting that we have it on promise from our Lord that the gates of hell will never prevail against the church (see Matt. 16:18). Is this a promise we can believe? Or will we, rather, become the very atheists we fear?

I realize that what I am saying is unsettling. I can hardly afford to be cavalier about these matters myself. After all, were Western society overturned, would I be able to receive grants from private foundations to write books? Would publishers be free to print them, especially if they are critical of the given social order or the reigning ideology? And as editor of a Christian magazine, would I be arrested? Would the magazine be shut down?

There is no doubt that we in the West are blessed with freedom. I am grateful to God for these privileges. Yet, we often forget that blessings can, because of our disobedience, become curses—as when freedom degenerates into license, as when material blessings are hoarded by those who ignore others in need. Let us be careful with freedom.

In our understandable quest to be blessed, we sometimes fall into shallow, self-serving notions of what it means to be blessed. We equate blessings with obvious, fairly routine things like a new sofa or a better job or the end of an illness. But we shouldn't stop there, lest we forget that exceptional blessings often result from suffering. We don't like to believe our Lord when He said, "Blessed are ye, when men shall revile you, and persecute you, and shall say all manner of evil against you falsely, for my sake" (Matt. 5:11).

In Berkeley in 1982, Bishop Basil of the Orthodox Church in America told a gathering about his imprisonment in a gulag in Yugoslavia during its Stalinist, *pre*-Titoist years. His suffering was what one would expect. Yet in his despair he was visited and comforted by St. Seraphim of Sarov in a dream, and he could say that during some of those days in the gulag, the barrier between this world and the world to come was gone. He experienced the ineffable, and thus not surprisingly, he reported that some of his days in prison were the happiest of his entire life.

THE TROUBLING QUESTION

Experiences like his may force us to ask the embarrassing question: is the West even especially Christian? Plenty of modern Manicheans insist that the West is Christian and the East godless and satanic. But the reality is far more complicated than that.

Any fair-minded and informed observer would probably have to concede that in many ways the United States is more corrupt than East Germany. It is not simply because we have a Mafia and they don't, that we have a thriving drug culture and they don't. They have no gay bars and bath houses, no salacious TV sitcoms, and no glorification of swinging singles or open marriage or bisexuality or sadomasochism.

The problem with the West, however, is broader than sex. The quest for sexual pleasure is but a segment of our quest for indiscriminate and unbridled pleasure of all sorts. Pleasure is not necessarily evil, of course, but it is the normal, predictable bait the devil uses to fuel our self-preoccupation and thus lead us into sin. The problem is our selfish preoccupation with pleasurable things—more precisely, treating other people as things, whether sexual or otherwise, to gratify or promote ourselves. This absorption with things is properly called materialism.

The Communist East has a *philosophical* materialism, which is obviously anti-Christian. But the West has a *practical* materialism, which goes largely unnoticed by Christians. How are we to choose between the East's materialism that may torment the body but leaves the soul relatively unscathed and the West's materialism that caresses the flesh to better devastate the soul?

We Western Christians are petrified by the prospect of being persecuted by the Eastern materialists, all the while remaining oblivious to the way we are being seduced by our own materialists. We would much rather be seduced than persecuted. Why? Not only because the thought of being persecuted is frightening but also because in our minds we have equated blessings with material goodies and comforts.

Few people are willing to admit the extent to which sexual permissiveness, drugs, the love of money, and careerism are wrecking the lives and families of millions of Christians in the West. It may be that Christians are better able to withstand the torments of the body than the seductions of the spirit. Certainly, the church is healthier when she stiffens her spine in the face of an openly declared enemy such as Marxism-Leninism than when she capitulates to an enemy disguised as a friend and called by the sweet names of Prosperity, Ease, and Freedom.

Here, precisely, is the rub: Christian anti-Communism deceives us because it gives permissive, materialistic capitalism a religious gloss and fails to alert us to the beguiling enemies in our midst who wish to domesticate the gospel into a friendly lapdog. Moreover, Christian anti-Communism lures us into assuming that Christians are, by divine right, destined to be rulers, thereby diverting us from facing the uncomfortable truth that, fundamentally, Christianity is much more about serving than ruling.

Let us heed the words and example of our Lord, who stressed that He "did not come to be served, but to serve" and that His followers should be animated by the same spirit (see Matt. 20:25-28 NASB).

A VIVID GLIMPSE
OF CHRIST'S "NEW MAN"

Even where [as in the West] Christ is accepted there is at the same time opposition to the full truth of...His Gospel. There is a desire to "reshape" Him, to...make Him fit in with the program of...consumerism. • *Karol Wojtyla*

Many of the East German Christians I talked with had had many opportunities to flee to the West before the Berlin Wall went up in 1961. But they didn't, largely because of what they saw as the greedy and salacious style of life in the West.

Observers have frequently noted that the Polish pope is repelled by the tone of life in the West. Whenever he denounces the philosophical materialism of the East, he seems to balance that criticism with a denunciation of the practical materialism—the consumerism—of the West. John Paul has commented that in the capitalist West "men have grown sick from too much prosperity and too much freedom."[1]

OUR DELIGHTFUL DISEASE

Most of us would probably nod our assent. Yet,

71

in reality, most of us Christians are so fearful of seeing our prosperity and freedom diminished or endangered in the slightest that we are willing to threaten the whole God-given world with nuclear incineration in order to keep alive those germs that feed our sickness.

Theologically conservative Christians are particularly likely to feel this way. Conservative Christians, who are correctly concerned that the churches have been abandoning their spiritual values, are usually the most materialistic Christians in regard to issues such as taxation, the domestic business climate, economic growth, our competitiveness in world markets, and our military posture in the world, which we rely on to defend our prosperity and freedom.

The United States has recently changed several environmental and health and safety regulations in favor of more profits and freedom for the privileged. Each day we hear and read about free enterprise methods that help us feather our own nests. Many biblically oriented Christians instinctively cheer such developments in American society. Obviously we don't really believe we have become sick from too much prosperity and freedom. The truth is that we Western Christians positively enjoy our sickness.

No wonder, then, we don't want to heed the warning of Karl Barth, when he said that

the continuance and victory of the cause of God...is not unconditionally linked with the forms of existence which it has had until now [in the West]. Yes, the hour may strike...when God, to our discomfiture, but to his glory...will put an end to this mode of existence because it lacks integrity and has lost its usefulness. Yes, it could be our duty to free ourselves inwardly from our dependency on that mode of existence even while it still lasts.[2]

Pope John Paul, Communism's gift to the church (a gift Communists wish they could somehow take back), tells us that while evangelization is the church's top priority, the church is the church of the poor and both God and His church have a special affection, a preference actually, for the poor.

This preference is not exclusive. The poor also include the poor in spirit. Yet the "church of the poor" is not a concept that may be relativized and spiritualized out of existence. For while Matthew records Jesus as saying, "Blessed are the poor in spirit" (5:3), Luke records Him as saying more simply, "Blessed be ye poor, for yours is the kingdom of God" (6:20).

Some of us who believe the Bible tells no falsehood have problems with the latter verse. Even if we are not particularly affluent in American terms, virtually all Americans are rich in global terms. If the kingdom of God belongs to the poor, what will happen to us on Judgment Day?

Not every Christian is called to be literally poor. But we are certainly called to be poor in spirit, which means more than being humble and meek. It means being indifferent to possessions and the allurements of the world, so that we are ready to become literally poor if a situation requires it. This proposition is easy to support in theory but terrifying in practice.

This is not a question of occasional alms. It is a question of the heart, for our treasure is where our heart is. And if we're constantly trying to "make it" or hang onto what we have (either personally or nationally), we can hardly claim to be poor in spirit.

Moreover, we'll never understand—never want to understand—what the Virgin Mary meant when she declared: "He hath scattered the proud in the imagination of their hearts. He hath put down the mighty from their seats, and exalted them of low degree. He hath filled the hungry with good things; and the rich he hath sent empty away" (Luke 1:51-53). For, as we assiduously pile up riches for ourselves on earth, we are, by our very passion to distance ourselves from those of low degree, letting it be known how much we abhor not only poverty but also the poor themselves.

Not all Christians are called to scarcity, but all are called to sanctity which, as Charles Williams asserted, is ultimately the only interesting thing in life. And as John Francis Kavanaugh has said, sanctity "will never be found where there is no sense of one's own personal poverty nor a corollary love of the poor."[3]

A NEW KIND OF LIGHT

One of the amusing things about returning to the States in 1966 was hearing the assumptions of many people. They thought we had been taken in by the Communists because we were young. Actually we went to East Germany with our eyes wide open so far as the severity of Communism was concerned. We didn't expect a utopia on a hill. Our disillusionment had little to do with how different

East Germany was from home and more to do with how *similar* it was.

But never mind. People would assume that since we had repudiated Marxism and accepted Christ and returned to the States, we had "seen the light"; and we would make testimonies to the truth of the American way, join the middle-class merry-go-round, and affirm the values of the local chamber of commerce. Ironically though, the light we did see in East Germany had nothing to do with the joys of prosperity. Rather, it was the light of Christ.

People didn't notice how little I had changed. All I had done was come to the awareness that Marxism does not have the truth about life, whereas Christianity does. Aside from the sheer realization that God exists and Jesus is His only Son, *I came to see that what I was looking for in Marxism could be found only in true Christianity.*

I had been looking for a "new man," a man infused with the spirit of solidarity with others, with a willingness to sacrifice his own interests and comforts for those of others, and with a sense of simplicity and modesty about his own place in the order of things. Most people do not manifest those traits, and that is certainly not my own natural bent. But in East Germany I had a vivid glimpse of what Jesus can do to transform people's lives, even to the point of personal inconvenience and peril. In this sense, then, I was forced to look upon East Germany the way Karl Barth did when he referred to it as "God's beloved (deeply beloved!) East Zone."[4]

Although persecution does not bring automatic

blessings to Christians, it can open up amazing opportunities for living the faith more fully. Christians have no business questing after martyrdom, but neither are we entitled to threaten the annihilation of humanity and God's creation in order to avoid the martyr's crown of thorns.

Jesus Christ is said to be love incarnate. I agree with this declaration, but let's be clear about what love is. It is not sentimentality or gullibility. Rather, God's love, though free, is a very demanding proposition. As Dorothy Day is well known for having said (quoting Dostoyevsky): "Love in action is a harsh and dreadful thing compared to love in dreams."

Love requires a willingness to sacrifice and even suffer, which is one reason Christians have always regarded sexual love outside the vows of marriage and outside the intention to have children as inauthentic. Jesus, though, as God, was rich, as a man became poor. There is no more awesome love than that the Creator of the universe should abase Himself at the hands of His trivial creatures, so that they might have the possibility of living eternally with Him. While Christ suffered so that we wouldn't have to suffer for our own iniquities, to love Him—to be truly grateful for what He did—is to want to be like Him. It is to "put...on the Lord Jesus Christ" (Rom. 13:14). It is to try to love as He loved and even to be willing to suffer as He did.

If we become like Him, we will learn about the cost of love, that it doesn't come cheaply. To be able to love is a sign of strength, not of weakness. The history of Christian sanctity reveals an integral connection between love and strength and suffering, so that we may speak of Christian love as the courage to suffer.

When we suffer, we learn not to take ourselves so seriously: we learn compassion for others. Jesus said: "As many as I love, I rebuke and chasten" (Rev. 3:19). The writer of Hebrews quoted the Old Testament, saying, "Despise not thou the chastening of the Lord, nor faint when thou art rebuked of him: for whom the Lord loveth he chasteneth, and scourgeth every son whom he receiveth." He then commented: "If ye endure chastening, God dealeth with you as with sons; for what son is he whom the father chasteneth not? But if ye be without chastisement...then are ye bastards, and not sons" (Heb. 12:5-8).

This is an ugly truth. The man who cannot love—like the spoiled child—is an illegitimate son. But the Lord chastens His sons, so that they "might be partakers of his holiness" (Heb. 12:10). Therefore we must be willing to accept chastisement, just as Jesus endured the "shame" of the cross and the "contradiction of sinners" (see Heb. 12:2, 3). Hence, to abhor suffering is to abhor authentic love.

Paul's hymn to love in 1 Corinthians 13 is unsurpassed ("And now abideth faith, hope, charity, these three; but the greatest of these is charity"). He knew well the blessings of adversity. He tells us he suffered a "thorn in the flesh," a harassing and painful ailment that he termed a "messenger of Satan" (2 Cor. 12:7). He prayed three times for God to take away the affliction, but God refused, saying, "My grace is sufficient for thee: for my strength is made perfect in weakness" (2 Cor. 12:9).

The affliction was actually a spiritual blessing, for it undercut Paul's natural inclination to be proud and conceited, which would have made him an ineffective evangelist and apostle. The affliction was precisely the way in which God acted mightily to protect Paul from dangers far greater than the affliction itself.

Paul was able to see his affliction as a privilege, and he was able to say what many East German Christians have come to say: "Therefore I take pleasure in infirmities, in reproaches, in necessities, in persecutions, in distress for Christ's sake: for when I am weak, then am I strong" (2 Cor. 12:10).

And Paul certainly knew persecution and suffering. Said he:

> Many a time [I have been] face to face with death. Five times the Jews have given me the thirty-nine strokes; three times I have been beaten with rods; once I was stoned; three times I have been shipwrecked, and for twenty-four hours I was adrift on the open sea....I have met dangers from...robbers, dangers from my fellow-countrymen, dangers from foreigners . . . dangers from false friends. I have toiled and drudged, I have often gone without sleep; hungry and thirsty, I have often gone fasting; and I have suffered from cold and exposure (2 Cor. 11:24-27 NEB).

If the plight of the East German Christians makes us tremble, we must remember that they are living in relative ease compared to what Paul endured for Christ's sake—or compared to what Christ endured for our sakes.

Paradoxically, Elena and I found it impossible to

become champions of America (where the church is suffocated with respectability) against Communism (where the church lives, as she first lived, in agony). It has been a peculiar position to be in: to reject Communism and yet to thank the Communists for taking the church seriously enough to attack her.

What a peculiar honor, therefore, it has been for East German Christians and dedicated Christians throughout history to be able to say with Paul:

> As God's servants, we try to recommend ourselves in all circumstances by our steadfast endurance. ...dying we still live on; disciplined by suffering, we are not done to death; in our sorrows we have always cause for joy; poor ourselves, we bring wealth to many; penniless, we own the world (2 Cor. 6:4, 9-10 NEB).

PUZZLING ALIGNMENT

My desire to disentangle Christianity from an uncritical allegiance to the West has another aspect, which is related to what I encountered when we returned to the United States in 1966. I returned a Christian, and I walked into an ever-escalating cultural revolution and the curious polarization surrounding it.

On one side were the radicals, children of the bourgeoisie, who were championing drugs and sexual licentiousness. On the other were those who "saw Red," those who viewed the debauch of our culture as simply one facet of a Marxist conspiracy to overturn all American institutions and values. Happily, most Christians resisted the cultural revolution, but not so happily, in doing that many felt they had to defend everything else the radicals were attacking: the "establishment," the structure of privilege and opportunity, the commercial ethic, the Vietnam War, and American military might. This alignment of forces puzzled me, for I could never quite figure out why the health of Christianity was tied up with the American way.

I take it as a given, then, that orthodox Christianity is clearly incompatible with Communist ideology. I also take it as a given that orthodox Christianity is antithetical to self-indulgence as epitomized by the sexual and drug revolutions. Numerous effective treatises have set forth strong biblical and theological arguments against these revolutions.

But relatively little has been done in Christian circles to show that an affirmation of traditional Christian sexual morality may well entail the adoption of a more critical stance toward both capitalism and the bourgeois lifestyle it often promotes. I will develop this idea throughout the following chapters.

PART TWO

A CULTURAL REVOLUTION

"I GOTTA HAVE IT NOW"

I knew they [my parents] loved me so much that if I cried I'd get my way, if I screamed I'd get my way, if I insisted I'd get my way. It was really total tolera-tion, total permissiveness....I'm really convinced that the whole of my recent activity in the move-ment [New Left] has been a playing out on a mas-sive political scale of the things I learned in the family. • *Jerry Rubin (1971)*

[Now] I'm into total money management, not only stock brokerage....Money is power. • *Jerry Rubin (1981)*

Masses of modern, Bible-believing Christians are drawn to organizations such as the Moral Ma-jority, which strive not only to restore traditional morality but also champion the entire range of so-called all-American values, from laissez-faire capi-talism to the middle-class success ethic to military brinksmanship. Before signing up with these Christian crusaders, one would be wise to examine carefully the roots of the American sexual revolu-tion, how capitalism and the sexual revolution have nurtured each other, and how middle-class values undergird that revolution.

Student radicals of the 1960s were the pioneers of the sexual revolution. Social scientists agree that the original student radicals tended to come from upper-middle-class homes, have parents with liberal sexual values, and be products of the permissive and nonpatriarchal child rearing characteristically practiced by the upper middle class. On the whole, student radicals were not in actual rebellion against their parents, as was widely thought at the time; rather they were striving to extend the personal permissiveness they learned from their parents and home environments to society in general.[1] They were remarkably successful.

Student radicalism has evaporated, but the lifestyles promoted by what was once called "the counterculture" have been legitimized by and assimilated into mainstream culture, especially upper-middle-class culture. Although the political thrust of the student New Left burned out, its cultural thrust continued on into the 1980s. Curiously, the delicate and superficial social idealism of the sixties was suffocated by the luxuriant flowering of "me-ism" in the seventies and early eighties, the roots of which go back to the radicalism of the sixties.

Students no longer riot and wave red flags. They are serious about their studies and preoccupied with career advancement. Yet there has been no rollback of the sexual revolution. As the historian Christopher Lasch put it, "Hostility to the family has survived the demise of the political radicalism of the sixties and flourishes amid the conservatism of the seventies."[2] Indeed, the "self-ism" of the conservative 1980s is the cultural revolution in full bloom, a revolution so durable that it lives on in spite of inflation, evangelical revivals, recession, shrinking public services, large-scale unemployment, AIDS, herpes, and (what to Christians is) the obvious emptiness of life without abiding commitment to others.

Of course, all revolutions grow old, or as their advocates would say, they "mature." For the media, the sexual revolution is no longer as new and "exciting" as it once was. Since just about every form of kinkiness has been tried, the sexual revolution has reached something of a plateau in the public mind.

But if the sexual revolution has found its natural saturation level, we must not lose sight of the fact that current sexual attitudes and practices are vastly different from what they were only two decades ago. And if the AIDS and herpes epidemics have made some people think twice before indulging themselves, we must not be so shortsighted as to think medical science will not one day soon discover cures for them.

The sexual revolution was made by the upper middle class, not the common people. Moreover, regardless of the intentions of some of the leading sexual revolutionaries, the revolution has not undermined American capitalism; it has actually strengthened its ethos. Moreover, American capitalism has provided libertine sexuality a very congenial environment in which to grow and thrive.

Consequently, the Moral Majoritarians in particular and politically conservative Christians in general need to re-examine their position. Promoting capitalist ideology may actually be an unproductive strategy for those interested in restoring traditional moral values. Furthermore, if we somehow managed to curtail expansionist world Communism, the cause of sexual and family morality would not be advanced in the slightest. In fact, the spread of Western values and institutions to Eastern Europe and the Soviet Union would make those areas more libertine, not less.

A FLASH FLOOD OF CHANGE

Because the quality of American life has changed so drastically, the term *revolution* is no exaggeration. As the sociologist Seymour Martin Lipset stated,

> If somebody in 1965 told me that...in but five years...there would be the kind of changes with respect to...homosexuals...women...and..."sexual permissiveness" that have occurred...I would have told them they were crazy. Such massive social changes do not occur that fast.[3]

But things that were indecent or unspeakable twenty years ago are now socially acceptable—in truth, *obligatory*—in many circles.

The American cultural revolution was occasioned by a decisive shift in attitudes toward the basic questions of life: What is right, and what is wrong? What is the purpose of our existence? The cultural revolution has discredited self-discipline, which is considered repressive and alienating, and it has legitimized and even glamorized self-indulgence, which is celebrated as liberating and self-authenticating.

The list of newly legitimate and nearly legitimate activities and attitudes is almost endless:

86

free love, swinging singles, living together, auto-eroticism, serial divorce, wife swapping, open marriage, birth control for the unmarried and for minors without parental consent, abortion, therapeutic fondling, homosexuality, bisexuality, sado-masochism, transvestitism, massage-cum-prostitution, public dances for hookers, public nudity, live sex shows, sex bars and bath houses, the androgynous and unisex look, sex role reversal, reverse sexual discrimination, marijuana and other drug abuse, and more. Except for the last mentioned, all these cultural phenomena are related to sex, and that is true because "nowhere have our public values—and perhaps even our private conduct—changed more noticeably than here."[4]

These phenomena cannot be conceived as being limited to isolated consenting adults; taken together they constitute a *social* revolution, a wrenching change in the rhythms, temperature, and mood of the social organism. Few individuals, however traditional their way of life, have been unscathed or untouched by these changes. The cultural revolution, the sexual and drug revolutions combined, has effected a massive shift in what counts as approved behavior.

SELF-GRATIFICATION

More than a cultural revolution is involved. The unifying theme of that revolution has been the exaltation of fun, the making of self-gratification into an end in itself. This preoccupation with self is manifest not only in obvious things such as advertising and self-oriented therapies but also in college curricula and popular religious culture.

The cultural revolution has swirled around sexual matters because the polymorphous powers of sex can be supremely self-gratifying, but used to be bottled up in the institution of marriage—heterosexual, monogamous, reproductive, and lifelong. The traditional family has been the primary enemy of the sexual revolution because the disintegration of the disciplines of family and marriage is prerequisite to the liberation of the primal self.

Artificial contraception has had something to do with these changes, but more important, for our discussion, than the existence of any technological innovation is what people decide to do—or allow themselves to do—with it. To be sure, artificial birth control can be used to revolutionize human relations by totally separating sex from love, commitment, and procreation. But even if one regards artificial contraception as inherently immoral, one must acknowledge that it has also been used to regulate the size of families and to space pregnancies. Therefore, while artificial birth control has both facilitated and accelerated the sexual revolution, it does not account for the revolution all by itself.

Secularization has had something to do with the revolution, but secularization has been advancing since the Enlightenment. Throughout the last two decades the United States has been, and still is, the most religious country in the Western world as measured statistically by people's assent to Judeo-Christian doctrines and attendance at worship services. And Communist countries, which are officially atheistic and rigorously secular, are far more traditional on cultural matters than the United States and the traditionally Christian nations of Western Europe. Therefore, we must look beyond the fact of secularization.

Nor was the cultural revolution simply a result of the Indochina war and resistance to the draft. It survived, and even extended itself, after their demise, and it has been experienced in advanced capitalist countries that had no military involvement in Indochina. The war and the draft produced widespread social alienation and thereby accelerated the pace of the cultural revolution and brought it into sharper focus, but the revolution was not merely an accidental by-product of such fortuitous circumstances.

What is most interesting sociologically is that the cultural revolution was originated by America's bourgeoisie. To be specific, it was born in the two key sectors of the upper middle class: the corporate elite with its higher level proprietors and managers, and the "New Class" of higher level professionals and technicians.

Although the corporate elite did not consciously set out to make a cultural revolution, the changes in the economy over which it has presided bear a unique responsibility for the revolution. Those who did intend to create a cultural revolution are to be found in the New Class. Within this class, which constitutes about half of the upper middle class, the most aggressive promoters of the revolution have been found among the intellectuals, those who create and/or disseminate abstract ideas, knowledge, and/or the artifacts of culture.

That the conscious creators of the revolution were intellectuals (and their shock troops, the apprentice intellectuals, most notably the student dissidents of the 1960s) does not mean, however, that it was the result of a single-minded imposition of ideas in a socioeconomic vacuum. Without an advanced capitalist context, their ideas would likely not have come to fruition.

Nevertheless, ideas *do* have consequences. While it is difficult to trace the influence of an idea with any rigor, the vulgar Marxist notion that ideas are impotent defies common sense. If editorialists didn't think ideas have consequences, they wouldn't editorialize, companies wouldn't advertise, pastors wouldn't preach, politicians wouldn't mount the hustings, and economic determinists wouldn't write books. People are usually free to reject efforts at persuasion, and the influence of ideas may be hastened or frustrated by other influences; but to conclude from this that ideas have no impact is unwarranted.

Throughout the Western world since at least the time of the Enlightenment (when intellectuals emerged as a sociologically identifiable group), intellectuals have had a reputation for being challengers of traditional verities and given social arrangements. In the area of culture and mores, they have had a reputation for bohemianism and antinomianism.

In the 1950s, the United States was culturally a rather traditional and consensual society, but significant pockets of intellectuals rejected that consensus. Indeed, according to the culturally radical literary scholar Morris Dickstein, the "immediate intellectual underpinnings" of the cultural revolution appeared in "the dissident works of the late fifties," particularly in the works of people such as Norman Mailer, Paul Goodman, Norman O. Brown, and Herbert Marcuse. These men may have been political and economic radicals, but as Dickstein said enthusiastically, "we knew that at bottom their gospel was a sexual one." Although their talk about sexual liberation was couched in elevated terminology, Dickstein allows that their message was probably about "just plain f---ing, lots of it."[5]

NURTURING THE REVOLUTION

The cultural revolution is now an established and seemingly irreversible social fact. Two factors go a long way in accounting for this situation.

First, its proponents occupy strategic positions in society, thereby exerting influence in excess of their numbers. They essentially control most of the leading cultural, educational, and mass media institutions of the land, institutions that have grown dramatically in size and importance as America has become more highly educated and technologically proficient.

Second, the changing nature of capitalism allowed the hedonistic sensibility of the intellectuals to come to fruition. This is the topic of the next two chapters, but a brief comment is in order here.

Beginning in the early decades of this century, the sheer productive capacity of capitalism has transformed the bulk of American society from a condition of scarcity to one of abundance. In the process, the ethos of our society was transformed. Previously, the great virtues were thrift, saving, self-restraint, and self-denial. But if those virtues had persisted in an age of abundance, capitalism would have had a tough time surviving.

Modern capitalism requires constant and immediate consumption. Supply characteristically overextends demand; therefore demand must be persistently stimulated by corporations themselves through advertising, which is often sexually suggestive. Because our economy thrives on high levels of consumption, of both products and experiences, capitalism now *requires* an ethos of self-indulgence. Self-denial impedes sales and depresses profits. Thanks to mass advertising, installment buying, and mass-marketing techniques, people can be coaxed into buying more and more.

The cultural revolution in general and the sexual revolution in particular are part and parcel of the I-gotta-have-it-now mentality that keeps the economy going and dismembers the family.

How often we used to hear that the family is the basic building block of society! It is hardly considered that anymore. It is no fluke that a nice avuncular man like the late John D. Rockefeller 3rd chaired a presidential commission that recommended birth control for unmarried youths and abortion on demand. JDR 3rd was not some starry-eyed freak; he knew what was good for corporate America over the long run. Significantly, he went on record as favoring what he called "experimental" approaches to marriage and family life, "open" attitudes toward sex, and "the discarding of stereotyped masculine and feminine roles." As he said of himself, "I am not given to errant causes."[6]

The capitalistic implications of the cultural revolution are vividly embodied in the colorful personality of Jerry Rubin, the archetypal flower child and former Yippie. The personification of the 1960s counterculture (he authored *Do It!*, a slogan that now lives forever in the ad copy churned out by Madison Avenue), he went on to sample the hip self-oriented therapies of the 1970s. In the 1980s he became unmistakably *le bourgeois gentilhomme.*

He was recently reported to be living in a "sleek Manhattan high-rise, complete with uniformed doorman," and married to a New York socialite. He has become a bona fide Wall Streeter—first as a well-paid venture banker for John Muir & Co. and then as head of his own private money management firm and Muir consultant. Of himself he said, "I'm very good at predicting trends," and in 1980 he predicted that "money and financial interest will capture the passion of the '80s."[7]

As of this writing he seems to be right, and the cultural changes he pioneered are in no small way responsible. For the sex and drug revolutions have transformed self-interest from a slightly suspect matter of fact into a liberating moral imperative. One can still hear investment counselor Rubin passionately advising his followers (now his clients) to "do it!"

Was the cultural revolution in America the result of some Bolshevik conspiracy? On the contrary, it was very much a home-grown product. Fundamentally, it grew out of a marriage of intellectual bohemianism with an economy increasingly requiring the liberation of all the desires of the primal self.

As the cultural revolution "matures" we may see an abatement of some of its more extreme manifestations, as certain of its excesses are tried and found wanting, and as victims of the revolution (e.g., children of divorced parents) yearn for more stability. For example, there have been some reports in the mid-1980s that youth are somewhat less permissive on some issues than were the youth of ten to twenty years ago. As the youth of the 1960s and 1970s enter middle age, a fresh "younger generation" is emerging. It would, however, be unwise at this point to make predictions about how this new generation's attitudes and behavior will jell once it arrives at adulthood. In any event, it would be foolish to expect the cultural revolution to be undone in the foreseeable future.

MORALITY AND
AMERICAN CAPITALISM

> There are people who want to keep our sex instinct
> inflamed in order to make money out of us. Be-
> cause, of course, a man with an obsession is a man
> who has very little sales resistance. • *C. S. Lewis*

Neoconservative critics of the cultural revolution have referred to the cultural revolutionaries,
the intellectuals, and their New Class allies as
composing an "adversary culture." According to
neoconservative thinking, the dominant intention
of the intellectuals and their allies is to subvert
not only our culture but also our economic system
of capitalism. This way of thinking is common to
most other schools of modern conservative
thought as well.

Neoconservatives, principally the journalist Irving Kristol and the sociologist Daniel Bell, argue
that the cultural revolution achieved by the adversary culture will ultimately undo capitalism itself.
The key factor in their analysis is that intellectuals
have undermined the legitimate cultural underpinnings of capitalism, without which capitalism
supposedly cannot survive.

According to Bell, our *economic* system demands delayed gratification, rationality, self-discipline, and efficiency, but our *cultural* life encourages sensuality, impulsiveness, and self-gratification. People are urged to "make it" financially but be "with it" culturally. These two imperatives are allegedly contradictory, and people are pulled in opposite directions.

Before the cultural revolution in America, however, the realms of work and culture were more or less in harmony, according to this view. At that time our culture called for self-restraint and circumspection, much like the economy did. But now that the two realms are allegedly in contradiction, trouble looms ahead for us. A liberationist culture is supposedly eating away at the rationale of the economy. Self-indulgence as a cultural norm is subverting the psychic reward structure that sustains capitalism.[1]

What we have lost is the work ethic, the willingness to deny oneself for the sake of one's work. Without this ethic, capitalism is said to lose its self-justification. According to Kristol, "capitalism at its apogee...[had] replaced all arbitrary (e.g., inherited) distributions of power, privilege, and property with a distribution that was directly and intimately linked to personal merit," namely, "frugality, industry, sobriety, reliability, piety."[2] His discounting of exploitation and of the continuing importance of inheritance and class stratification involves a romanticization of capitalism, of course.

Without the work ethic, argue Bell and Kristol (both of whom are religious Jews), capitalism loses all "transcendental"[3] or moral justification, for which hedonism is no substitute. On a social level, then, capitalism is morally naked, and on a personal level, individuals are supposedly sapped of their will to produce and achieve.

Both Bell and Kristol were leaders of the neoconservative movement in the 1970s. But Kristol moved to the right to become a rather unabashed defender of the free-market style of capitalism. On the other hand, Bell, favoring a mixed capitalist economy, held himself aloof from the rightward trend of most other neoconservatives. Nevertheless, both Bell and Kristol are joint critics of the cultural revolution. In that, obviously, I do not resist them. But they have unwisely tied in their critique with a defense of the prevailing economic order. In so doing, they have allowed themselves to become leaders of a widespread pro-capitalist backlash that feeds the moral, cultural disease they themselves despise.

HEDONISM AND CAPITALISM

I would argue that hedonism and modern capitalism are not necessarily contradictory. In fact, many patriotic American Christians are embarrassed that the two seem to be walking hand in hand today.

Nothing prevents a person's being self-restrained on the job but devil-may-care on the weekends or at lunch. The business world was reveling in the three-martini, three-hour lunch long before Hugh Hefner came on the scene. Such behavior is usually referred to as "unwinding" and "blowing off steam."

Actually, because money buys so many pleasures, people are still motivated to work hard and try to move up the economic ladder. The more money one earns, the more one can buy pleasure or the things that give pleasure.

This is no idle consideration. Pleasure can be habit-forming. What gives pleasure today often produces boredom tomorrow.

Certainly, there is no reason why the motivation to make money must necessarily be weakened by an inflamed desire for pleasure. Indeed, the passion for pleasure can incite the passion for money. Not surprisingly, the combination of hard work and hard play has reportedly become fashionable among career people. According to Christian psychologist Paul C. Vitz, "Millions of individuals are attempting to find heroic meaning in the private neuroses of their personal careers. They fantasize tough-minded accomplishment surrounded by the soft rewards of various pleasures: stoical existentialism at work, epicurean consumerism at play."[4]

Moreover, it is historically fallacious to separate moneymaking from pleasure, as if they had nothing in common. The sober Puritans and Calvinists, those theological forerunners of capitalist society, abjured every worldly pleasure except the pleasure of making money—and their grandchildren would discover the pleasure of spending it.

Historians usually argue that capitalism would not have developed when it did were it not for the Protestant Reformation's discrediting of the Catholic ban on usury (a ban grounded in the Old and New Testaments and the teachings of the church fathers). Strictly speaking, usury is taking money, or charging interest, for borrowed money over and above the principal. More generally, usury is the taking of an exorbitant amount of interest on a loan.

Usury was connected historically to the precapitalist sin of *luxury*, a word which in archaic English usage meant "lasciviousness" or "lust." Hence, Chaucer could write in 1386 of the "foule lust of luxurie." In the German language, one translation for "luxuriant" is *wuchernd*, which derives from the verb *wuchern*, meaning "to grow wildly or rankly." The German *wuchern* and the Latin *luxuria* have the same meaning: they originally come from descriptions of vegetation and mean "rank growth" or "to grow rankly or without restriction." The principal substantive form of *wuchern* is *Wucher*, which means "usury."

Although we no longer think in terms of the equivalence of sensual and financial enjoyment, the ancient concept of luxury reveals the connection. Lustful sexual activity as well as exorbitant moneymaking, money spending, and interest taking should be understood in terms of *luxuria*.[5] As a result, we cannot be satisfied with facile distinctions between hedonism and the spirit of capitalism.

Christians must not be mystified that the same Jesus who said, "Whosoever looketh on a woman to lust after her hath committed adultery with her already in his heart" (Matt. 5:28), also said, "Lend, expecting nothing in return" (Luke 6:35 NASB).

As creatures of an interest-ridden capitalist society, we can hardly bear the thought that the taking of interest might be as bad as lust. But we dare not forget that the problem of usury is only one aspect of a more consuming problem: the love of money, itself a form of lust. For Paul stated, "They that will be rich fall into...many foolish and hurtful lusts....For the love of money is the root of all evil" (1 Tim. 6:9–10).

Contrary to Bell's and Kristol's views, hedonism has not cut the link between industriousness and financial reward. The 1970s and 1980s have seen the institutionalization of the cultural revolution alongside a renewed interest in making money and enjoying the good things in life. Those of us steeped in the Bible and Christian tradition will not be surprised that an increasingly serious attitude toward personal economic gain has gone hand in hand with a continuing quest for pleasure.

INDIVIDUALISM

Contrary to Bell's and Kristol's assertions, capitalism has no need for traditional Judeo-Christian morality. All it needs is an atmosphere where the wants of the individual are self-validating. The individualism fostered by the women's liberation movement, sexual freedom, abortion on demand, and the drug culture works to reinforce many of the working assumptions of capitalism.

One need only peruse the narcissistic manifestos written on behalf of sexual liberation, women's liberation, and self-realization—slogans such as "I gotta be me" and "looking out for number one"—to understand that self-indulgence is widely perceived as a positive moral good in society. That our culture now encourages people to pursue their own pleasure with abandon can be and is seen as morally good.

Today, apologists for what under the sway of Christendom would have been called "immoral-ity" argue that they are actually promoting a higher morality—a new morality for a new society. It seems our society is groping toward a new moral norm aptly expressed in the words of *The New Yorker*'s Brendan Gill: "The first rule of life is to have a good time; and the second rule...is to hurt as few people as possible in the course of doing so. There is no third rule."[6]

This is the morality of "consenting adults"— adults should be able to do whatever they want, however twisted or debased, as long as nonconsenting individuals are not involved or harmed. According to this view, we live in a pluralistic society, and freedom of choice in morality is freedom enhancing and therefore morally preferable to a tradition-bound society that constrains such choice. Indeed, traditional virtues are dismissed as unhealthy hang-ups and forms of bondage.

Thanks to this new hedonistic morality, individualism is thriving in America as never before. We are, as conservative author Tom Wolfe recognizes, in the midst of "the greatest age of individualism in American history."[7]

American individualism may be rooted historically in the desire to protect private enterprises from external interference, but our cultural revolution has extended this liberty to the private conduct of individuals. In this sense, the cultural revolution is a flowering of the spirit of capitalism—and, conversely, the renewed spirit of enterprise we've witnessed recently is a flowering of the cultural revolution.

Liberty is not absolute in either realm, of course, but there is now actually a congruence between both the economic and private realms.

SELF-INDULGENCE

The writer Susan Sontag revealingly noted in 1969 that "American radicals are claiming one of the fundamental promises of American society-...selfishness."[8] Most radicals of the 1960s would have repudiated that judgment, preferring to believe that they were combating selfishness and that American capitalism would not be able to survive the revolution in culture they were spearheading. For example, Richard Flacks argued that the cultural changes inspired by the New Left "cannot be contained within a capitalist framework."[9]

But on this point the radicals were mistaken in their optimism, as are Bell and Kristol in their pessimism. The radicals misjudged their declared enemy—capitalism—and played right into its hands.

The radicals did not realize how deeply American were the norms to which they were appealing; they had no idea how flexible American capitalism is. Nor, indeed, did they see that their revolution was, objectively, deeply bourgeois.

Of course, *bourgeois* is a slippery word. Few people are proud to call themselves bourgeois; not even the actual bourgeoisie—the upper middle class—uses the term. The word seems to have a generally pejorative connotation. But not with Bell and Kristol who speak admiringly of bourgeois virtues, such as self-discipline, delayed gratification, and restraint.[10]

The great difficulty with calling these virtues bourgeois is that they are, in large measure, no longer characteristic of the bourgeoisie. Indeed, Bell is forced to admit that "bourgeois culture vanished long ago."[11]

When Bell suggests that we have capitalism without a bourgeois culture, he strains credibility. A more felicitous way of defining *bourgeois* would be to say that, by and large, bourgeois *is* as bourgeois *does*. If the bourgeoisie—the corporate elite and the New Class, which together constitute the upper middle class—is now "into" self-indulgence instead of self-restraint, then we should say that self-indulgence and immediate gratification are the bourgeois virtues today.

Perhaps the true contradiction of capitalism was between the "liberating" potential of private property and its "puritanical" superstructure of bygone days. Cultural self-restraint may have impeded the further development of the capitalist order, and thanks to the cultural revolution, that impediment has been stripped away. Indeed, it is likely that so-called "puritanical repression" was fundamentally antagonistic to the bourgeois sensibility but temporarily unavoidable under conditions of economic scarcity.

There is continuity between the new bourgeois values and certain old ones. Personal freedom in the economic marketplace is an old bourgeois value, and it remains fundamentally intact today. Actually, the characteristically bourgeois emphasis on economic self-enrichment has been extended to the cultural marketplace today, blossoming forth as self-indulgence.

The bourgeois virtues of self-restraint referred to by Bell and Kristol are still alive and well in the working class and lower middle class. We would be more accurate now in speaking of self-restraint as a *working-class* virtue.

Once these matters of definition are settled, we can see the importance of understanding the cultural revolution, having been made by the bourgeoisie on behalf of radically bourgeois values, as bourgeois, not antibourgeois. Once we grasp this concept, we realize why public opinion analyst Everett C. Ladd, Jr. reported in 1978 that in America "property is not a besieged value"[12]—indeed, why capitalism is not in peril at all.

The private property system is remarkably supple, and all the drastic cultural changes of the last twenty years have been accomplished without tampering with the corporate structure. Indeed, there is no reason why these changes must lead to socialization of industry or redistribution of income and wealth in favor of common people.

Capitalism and hedonism are mutually dependent and supportive today. American capitalism has shifted from a work ethic to a consumption/gratification ethic, with the materialistic spirit abiding. The point of achieving material success is no longer to prove one's favor in the sight of God or one's moral uprightness in the eyes of one's community. Rather, success has come to mean making lots of money in order to spend and enjoy it oneself. The common refrain is, "I want more for *me.*"

THE SPIRIT OF
CONSUMERISM

The individual serves the industrial system...by consuming its products. On no other matter, religious, political or moral, is he so elaborately and skillfully and expensively instructed. • *John Kenneth Galbraith*

The primary purpose of the corporation is to sell its products. But it is one thing to produce goods and services and another to see that they are actually bought.

Quite naturally, therefore, products are advertised in terms of the enjoyment, convenience, satisfaction, and sheer pleasure they afford. Enjoyment is nothing to be sneered at, after all. And yet, the overall ethos of consumerist capitalism implies that pleasure is self-justifying and always to be maximized.

Furthermore, selling thrives on change in style, taste, and standards. Advertising defines new needs and creates new fashions. Capitalism, like journalism, thrives on novelty; both are driven to institutionalize the avant-garde.

The more affluent the society, the more effective advertising can be. As John Kenneth Galbraith notes, "The further a man is removed from physical need the more open he is to persuasion—or management—as to what he buys."[1] In such a situation, ascetic habits of the past had to be made subservient to the corporate system. People had to be instructed on the legitimacy of letting go of their values and realizing their wildest, most hidden desires. Hence, the value of self-restraint had to be undermined, and historically it was the advertising system that accomplished this objective.

GOOD-BY NEEDS, HELLO WANTS

A spirit of consumerism—"grabbing all I can"—is good for our highly developed economy. Unlike the early, Horatio Alger-type capitalism of scarcity, the problem now is not how to keep supply equal to the demand for necessities but how to jack up demand to equal the supply of non-necessities. When demand slackens, goods and services go unbought, profits plunge, workers are thrown out of jobs, and capitalism runs the risk of collapse.

Curiously, since the consumerist-hedonist ethos helps ensure that goods and services will be bought, capitalism has emerged from the cultural revolution, all other things being equal, healthier than ever. When capitalism existed in a situation of economic scarcity, it required an ethic of hard work, sacrifice, and delayed gratification. Now that it exists in a situation of economic abundance, it requires an ethic of self-indulgence. Hence, capitalism is driven not only to whet appetites but also to commercialize unusual forms of indulgence.

Thus, as its productive engine has expanded beyond the output of necessities, capitalism has developed an interest in "breaking down all traditional social bonds in favor of the bonds generated by the productive apparatus."[2]

In seeking to intensify the authority of commercial suggestion and enhance the ideology of personal pleasure, advertisers have been quick to use whatever forces are antagonistic to the morality of self-restraint and are capable of undermining the authority of the traditional family. They have happily come to appropriate the vocabulary, attitudes, and images of the New Left, the sexual revolution, women's liberation, and even drug-induced esthetics.

But regardless of the pitch, advertising inherently compromises family solidarity "by inculcating a consumer ethic which entices families onto a debilitating and distracting financial treadmill and by enticing them also to their separate pleasures, in comparison with which family activities appear boring and insignificant."[3] Currently, for example, business is discovering that a large, fashion-minded and affluent homosexual market has gone largely untapped. The cultivation of that market could turn out to be a key factor in ultimately legitimizing homosexuality socially and guaranteeing the success of gay liberation politically.

SUBTLE SELLING

One of the best ways of selling people things they don't really need is to market images, to reinterpret the customer's identity in the light of some new good or service, to convert luxuries into psychic necessities. You may not need an expensive foreign sports car, for instance, but your ego needs some tender loving care. So you buy the car. The point is not so much owning a certain car with particular mechanical features as it is purchasing the image of being fashionable and visibly successful. The proud owner of the car becomes a new person whose very gait and glow communicate self-assurance.

Madison Avenue also selects and processes current ideas that are gaining acceptance and then glorifies them. Women's liberation provides a classic case in point. Jim Hougan cited a perfume ad as an example. The ad went roughly as follows: "You're a liberated woman and you don't care about marriage. You boldly tell your 'man' as much." Will this put him off? Oh no, for "you're wearing our perfume." The result? "He pulls out the ring and places it on your finger. No ordinary ring, it's five carats!" The obvious message is that liberated women can have their ideological cake and eat it too, that women's liberation is truly chic. Not to accept women's liberation—or at least its rhetoric—is to be a hopeless clod.

The perfume company in question has been selling not only perfume but ideology, and, in so doing, striking a mightier blow for women's liberation than a multitude of manifestos and consciousness-raising sessions. In a sense, this company has peddled women's liberation more effectively than perfume. Women may decide rationally that they don't care for the company's perfume, but since the subject of the ad was perfume, the ideological message was hardly noticed and thus absorbed without adequate reflection. It was accepted subliminally.

Hence, declared Hougan (with approval!), women's consciousness was "subverted" rather than "convinced." Hougan, who is an apologist for such things, said accurately that Madison Avenue is "both the machinery of our decadence and its first line of defense."[4]

Another example of a mighty blow struck for this type of "liberation" was one sports car ad that went something like this: A sophisticated-sounding woman said, "When I was twenty-five I drove a station wagon. But I'm no longer married, and my kids are now grown. All that is just a rusted memory. Now I have a career....And you should see my red convertible....Now when I see those ladies in their station wagons full of kids and dogs and groceries, I wave at them from my new car and say, 'There but for the grace of my convertible go I.' "

FANTASY: A PERSISTENT CULPRIT

Long before the 1960s, big business employed motivational researchers to probe people's sexual anxieties, fixations, and fantasies. This inquiry has paid rich dividends, and sex has been used to peddle just about everything. As a not-too-surprising result, people's actual attitudes have shifted to match the fantasies in which they are constantly being invited to participate.

Consider a few of the potent ways in which corporations have legitimized sexual permissiveness: "All my men wear English Leather" pitches one ad, "or they wear nothing at all." Or there's the Swedish blonde seductively cooing, "Take it off, take it *all* off" at the man shaving with Noxzema. Or, Brooke Shields coyly spreads her legs and says, "You know what comes between me and my Calvins? Nothing."

Advertising can use sex to glamorize the business ethic itself. For example, an ad for *American Business* magazine featured a solicitation from a very attractive woman, saying: "DARLING: I like men who like money—who know how to get it, enjoy it. I'm betting you're one of them, and I'd like to give you a subscription to a magazine that's SINFULLY enriching." What the ad was saying is not only that the magazine is a key to success in business but also that successful businessmen get to enjoy attractive women.

Advertising has cast an approving gloss on other facets of the cultural revolution—even drug use. One of the most blatant uses of a drug-related theme in an ad was for Yves Saint Laurent's Opium perfume. A lavishly bejeweled blonde in oriental costume was apparently in the midst of an opium dream, and the come-on, in relatively obscure but very fashionable French, was perfect: "OPIUM....pour celles qui s'adonnent à Yves Saint Laurent" (for those who are addicted to Yves Saint Laurent).

Thanks to the legitimizing function of Madison Avenue, which helped pave the way for the cultural revolution and facilitated its triumph, the moral upheaval of recent years was accomplished with amazing swiftness, justifying the use of the word *revolution*. Even partisans of that revolution, such as Morris Dickstein, were amazed by its rapid and widespread success. In 1977 he said, "I'm still astonished that pornography can be freely circulated in this country, that abortion and birth control are publicly accepted rights."[5]

Without the presence of consumerist capitalism to instruct citizens on the appropriateness of letting go of both scruples and dollars, and without the power of advertising to do the instructing, bohemianism would most likely still be confined to enclaves like Greenwich Village and North Beach.

THE LEFTIST CONSUMERS

If modern capitalism liberates the private vices, it is strange, even scandalous, to see socialists and progressives *in the West* fall all over each other promoting cultural revolution—as though smoking hashish, having orgies in dorms, trying out sadomasochism, and integrating restrooms sexually had something to do with overcoming or reforming capitalism. What actually results is the average person's tendency to associate progressivism in general with the eccentric and bizarre.

This phenomenon is not recent. In 1937 George Orwell, himself a socialist, remarked that "one sometimes gets the impression that the mere words 'Socialism' and 'Communism' draw towards them with magnetic force every...nudist ...sex maniac...'Nature Cure' quack...and feminist in England."[6]

The socialistic logic of controlling economic activity justifies controlling private activity as well. The notion that what consenting adults do in private has no social effect is fiction. Logically, collectivists should be the first to realize that when enough consenting adults harm themselves, physically or emotionally, the result is a social problem, regardless of whether consent was involved.

Leftists have reached the point where either

111

they reappropriate the ordinary family virtues of the common people or they utterly surrender themselves to the bourgeois spirit. Jarvis Tyner, a black American radical, was asked in the late 1960s if it was all right for radicals to "punish the system" and enrich the "movement" by engaging in shoplifting. No, he said poignantly, all that would do is spoil the "dignity of the struggle." I was surprised at the time, and impressed.

That so many Western socialists have gone lusting after the gods of bourgeois self-indulgence has spoiled the dignity of socialism, as that term is understood in the West. To be sure, socialism is about "more," having more of the good things in life, but socialism has historically been about more than "more." It has been about human dignity, a concept rooted in the Incarnation. "Having" is not an end in itself; it is, or should be, a prelude to "being" more. "Having" is only a precondition for more important pursuits, and when it gets in the way of those pursuits, it is to be avoided.

Irving Kristol once quipped that when confronted with a teen-age stripper, the only question an American leftist would ask would be, "Is she paid the minimum wage?" If the socialist or leftist will not ask about the dignity of the human person and of the human body, if he will not ask about the nobility of youth, if he will not ask about what it means for human relations to commercialize and impersonalize love and sex, if he will not ask about the impact on the family and families to come, then socialism and progressivism have lost their moral vision. Apparently, most leftists these days don't want to ask these kinds of questions. According to socialist Erazim Kohák,

The Spirit of Consumerism

The economic achievements of socialism, social welfare legislation, progressive taxation, trade unionism, [and] industrial democracy are all well and good, but without a moral vision they too become only a collective egocentrism.

Kohák goes on: "How can we regain...the self-realization by self-transcendence toward a moral ideal" that makes a decent society possible?[7]

Che Guevara is celebrated for having made the improbable statement that revolutionaries can be motivated by love. Socialism is supposed to be about being free to regard one's neighbor with love rather than with fear or envy, about the priority of cooperation over competition. Therefore, socialism should be about feeling free to give as well as receive.

If love is important in society, it is even more important in face-to-face relationships. Although we may profess to love humankind, we may find it difficult to love particular humans. Love is not just a momentary, gushy feeling. If it is real, it involves commitment, which inevitably entails suffering. That's the pinch.

And yet, we gladly suffer those we love, for that is the nature of love. In a sense, it should be easier to love, and sacrifice for, a particular loved one with a unique face and personality, one who can return love for love, than to do so for an abstraction such as "humanity" or "the people." If one cannot enter into loving relationships on a small scale, such as in one's family, what likelihood is there that one's professed love of humanity will amount to anything at all?

If leftists believe that in interpersonal relations

113

love is ephemeral and only self-love is durable, the same logic dictates that self-interest should govern economic relations. If we are discouraged from harnessing our self-will in interpersonal relations, what makes us think we will feel encouraged to do so in public relations?

Modern leftists, who talk glibly about creating a more loving society, have been woefully negligent in cultivating and nurturing authentic love where it is actually found—in the most natural of human associations, the family. Claiming to love humanity is too often an alibi for avoiding the forbearance and pain involved in loving real people.

Leftists in the West have often been in the forefront of efforts to dissolve the too-often tenuous bonds of love that unite actual persons. They have been outspoken promoters of sex for sale (legalized pornography and prostitution) and of the deregulation of abortion and divorce. They have winked at the glamorization of promiscuity and have readily approved efforts to legitimize homosexual liaisons, which are chronically transient. Strangely, leftists have surrendered sex to the capitalist spirit by allowing sex to become a commercial transaction, a self-centered calculation, a momentary atom of pleasure, a way in which one person uses another.

In the West, the Left has concocted a rationale for sexual self-indulgence, while the capitalist Right has established a rationale for material self-indulgence. These two rationales are but two sides of the same coin: consumerism. This spirit of self-absorption seems all-pervasive in the West now.

Is there a Christian way out?

114

PART THREE

A CHRISTIAN RESPONSE

GETTING TO KNOW
COMMON PEOPLE

Aside from economic issues, perhaps nothing grieves the worker so much as the contempt universally displayed in our society for his culture. • *Patricia Cayo Sexton and Brendan Sexton*

If the cultural revolution was made to order for the upper middle class, the highly educated business and professional people, one would expect to see evidence of it in public opinion polls. These polls would show that upper-middle-class people have been more receptive to libertine values than have the common people. And this is indeed the case. In fact, specific terms have been coined to symbolize this phenomenon, such as "limousine liberals" and, more recently, "yuppies" (young, upwardly mobile professionals).

WHAT THE POLLS SHOW

A 1969 *Newsweek*-Gallup poll, taken at the height of the counterculture years, found 72 percent of the poor agreeing that the emphasis on sex and nudity in movies, theaters, books, and magazines was undermining the nation's morals a great deal. Only 58 percent of the wealthy felt that way.[1]

On the question, "Would you turn in your son or daughter if found possessing marijuana in his or her room?" Harris surveys in the early 1970s revealed that 57 percent of those with incomes below $5,000 would, but only 27 percent of those in the $15,000-and-over bracket would.[2]

Although the marijuana issue is largely a matter of generations (older people are considerably more negative about its use than younger people), class differences are evident among young people: a 1970 Gallup poll found that 58 percent of college students whose parents' income was $15,000 and above favored the legalization of marijuana, whereas 42 percent of those whose parents' income was below $7,000 agreed.[3] A 1972 University of Michigan survey found 41 percent of college-educated adults favoring legalization, but only 19 percent of adults with a high school education favored it.[4]

Pollsters generally agree that, for whatever reason, variation in education accounts for more of the variance in percentages on cultural issues than does variance in occupation or income. But the fact that low educational standing usually goes hand in hand with low occupational standing and low income means that this distinction is of negligible consequence.

On a 1980 question, "If a draft were to become necessary, should young women be required to participate as well as young men?" Gallup found 62 percent of business and professional people saying "should," but only 45 percent of manual workers agreed.[5]

118

According to a 1974 Gallup survey, only 48 percent of manual workers favored legalized abortion through the first trimester, but 66 percent of business and professional people did.[6] According to a 1977 Gallup survey, 31 percent of business and professional people said abortion should be legal under any and all circumstances, but only 17 percent of manual workers felt that way.[7]

Polls conducted by the National Opinion Research Center (NORC) between 1972 and 1977 found 26 percent of high-school-educated adults saying adultery is "not always wrong" and 44 percent of the college-educated upper middle class saying so. In the same polls 26 percent of high-school-educated adults said homosexuality is "not always wrong," but 52 percent of the college-educated upper middle class said so.[8]

Where the business and professional components of the upper middle class are clearly distinguished by pollsters, business people alone show up as more culturally libertine than workers. For example, regarding the question of whether admitted homosexuals should be free to teach in schools, propagate their views through public speaking, and disseminate their advocatory books in public libraries, a 1976 NORC survey found 66 percent of professionals, 52 percent of business people, and only 36 percent of manual workers in agreement.[9]

These responses, which are typical of surveys taken throughout the last twenty years, reflect class divisions on cultural issues. Not all the available evidence points in the direction cited here, but most of it does. Public opinion analyst Everett C. Ladd, Jr. finds the overall evidence for such divisions to be "consistent and perceptible" and "as dramatic as one could ever expect to find" when dealing with "often 'mushy' survey data."[10]

In our own circles of friends and acquaintances, we may know of people who do not fit these statistical tendencies—affluent people whose cultural values are traditional, blue-collar workers who are libertine—but they are exceptions to undeniable sociological patterns.

There is, then, a clear-cut and significant tendency for cultural libertinism to increase as one goes up the occupational, income, and educational ladders, so much so that one may speak generally of a cultural/moral form of class struggle between the upper middle class and the common people.

In fact, we often hear members of the educated upper middle class wax poetic about the culture of Sioux Indians, Chinese peasants, Gypsies, and Eskimos, and decry the Americanization or Westernization of other cultures as forms of cultural imperialism. But no such solicitude is shown toward the metal worker, the plumber, or the auto mechanic in our own native land. On the contrary, the cultural imperialism of the new morality is perpetrated on these absurd creatures with impunity.

To disdain the metal worker is to disdain not only his culture but also to disdain *him*. The actress Shirley MacLaine epitomized this connection when she said, "I don't believe in conventional marriage. If convention made me and the people I love happy, I'd be conventional. But the people I love are not conventional."[11]

Common people proclaim with utter sincerity that they're proud to be common ordinary Americans. But beneath these protestations is a gnawing awareness that the best and the brightest aren't at all impressed.[12]

Common people seem to feel ambivalent about their place in the social structure. They're quite human. Sure they would like to be able to stick their noses up in the air. Of course they would like to triple their incomes and have prestigious jobs, a summer house, winter holidays in the Caribbean, a maid, a new car every year, a son at Yale and a daughter at Vassar (or maybe, vice versa).

And then again...they wouldn't. To have all those things—and it is the human condition to fantasize about how delectable they would be—would make them into different, alien people. For to change one's way of life is to change one's identity, one's self.

Since the common man does indeed value his commonness, however hesitantly, he is often put off by successful people who are visibly taken with their own success, swollen with themselves. Moreover, he may suspect there is a price to be paid for moving up in the world, namely, a loss of the "virtues of family devotion and shared time with wife, children and relatives."[13] This consideration is vital, because working-class life tends to be family-centered.

TRADITION AND THE WORKING CLASS

As I have already posited, working-class culture is characteristically tradition-bound. A common man's hero is one who accepts "the validity of traditional virtues, such as 'wholesomeness,' and traditional institutions, such as religion."[14] Working-class morality is dominantly "ascetic" and characterized by a concern for "control against impulsiveness."[15] Not surprisingly, working-class sensibility (unlike that of the upper middle class) stipulates that "school is a place where teachers are expected to be tough disciplinarians; where children are expected to behave respectfully and to be punished if they do not."[16]

The traditional cultural outlook of the commoner is predicated in large measure on family upbringing, financial well-being, and education.

1. Since common people are usually brought up in families where propriety and obedience to conventional norms are stressed, they are not as inclined to adopt an experimental lifestyle as are upwardly mobile and affluent people.

2. Affluence gives people the economic security and oportunity to experiment with their self-identities, enlarge their range of sensual and cerebral experiences, and unbutton their inhibitions. Upper-middle-class people can literally *afford* to go through adult identity crises and experiment with sex, drugs, and exotic self-improvement cults in pursuit of self-realization. Life can be seen as a kaleidoscope of possibilities. One almost owes it to oneself "to try dried grasshoppers with his martinis and the equivalent with his sex, his...child rearing, and all else."[17] Common people, not prone to this lifestyle to begin with, do not usually have the financial resources to afford it.

3. Since the commoner has had much less exposure to higher education and the liberal arts, he does not have the questioning frame of mind that would lead him to want to rearrange his psyche (unless he picks it up from the mass media).

Higher education is said to open up new worlds, to put one in a position to see things from differing vantage points. Of course, higher education is valuable and not to be denigrated; it is an indispensable ingredient for healthy social change. Yet, on cultural questions, the questioning frame of mind prevalent on campuses is usually tilted in only one direction. Old orthodoxies are ridiculed, and inverse orthodoxies often take their place.

As much as one imbibes a critical spirit in college, one all too often also imbibes an *un*critical attitude toward cultural relativism and toward the hedonism that often results from it. It has been statistically demonstrated, for example, that college tends to turn students away from traditional sexual morality and religion, to decrease the feminine qualities of females and the masculine qualities of males, and generally increase hedonistic attitudes.[18] Furthermore, these changes tend to persist after the students have left college.[19]

While education opens up new worlds, it does not usually open students up to the world of the working class. Educator James Q. Wilson notes that "the purpose of a liberal arts education is to induct a student, however partially and briefly, into the world of the intellectual,"[20] which is manifestly not a world of working-class cultural values.

The common man is characteristically concerned with family solidarity, propriety, making a living, and the proposition that men should be masculine and women feminine. While he desires a better standard of living, he is usually "not attracted to the middle class style of life with its accompanying concern for status and prestige."[21]

This has not deterred Madison Avenue, however,

from trying to turn workers into compulsive consumers. One would have to be a virtual monastic to resist the lure of consumerism, and so one sees in working-class life what social scientists S. M. Miller and Frank Riessman call the "excitement" theme, that fascination with gadgets and other tangible goods that is "often in contradiction with" the worker's traditional morality.[22]

The consequence of such consumerism is to give the commoner the sensation that he is not so common after all. He is special, he has arrived, and he is part of the middle class.

This consumerism, with its promise of *individual* pleasure, convenience, and thrills, has been, historically, a subtle and very seductive form of cultural aggression perpetrated against working-class family life, culture, and solidarity. But more than that, it was the opening wedge of the bourgeois cultural revolution, which is a less subtle assault on working-class family life, culture, and solidarity.

FEMINISM AGAINST THE WORKING CLASS

Perhaps the major example of the cultural revolution's rape of working-class culture has been the women's liberation movement. As a movement, women's liberation had its origins in the New Left, the upper-middle-class youth movement of the 1960s. Women's liberation quickly spread from New Left environs to the adult New Class in particular and the upper middle class in general, where both men and women were already giving up on the idea that the male is the head of the household and that there is a clear distinction between what is masculine and what is feminine.

Indeed, young New Leftists were merely extending to greater lengths the values they had already learned in their upper-middle-class homes. According to social scientist Richard Flacks, "having seen their parents share authority and functions more or less equally...these were boys who did not understand masculinity to mean physical toughness...and girls who did not equate femininity with passivity and domesticity."[23]

Business got into the act when it recalled that feminism can have cash value. In the 1920s, the tobacco industry had appropriated the feminism of that decade to induce women to take up cigarette smoking. To get women to smoke could double sales. Cigarettes were construed as "torches of freedom," marks of liberation from the taboo that women should not smoke, a theme Virginia Slims ads ("You've come a long way, baby") continue to play upon. By the mid-1920s, advertisers had "ventured pictures of pretty girls imploring men to blow some smoke their way; and by the end of the decade billboards boldly displayed a smart-looking woman, cigarette in hand."[24]

Now commercials and ads routinely feature liberated women engaged in activities previously considered masculine. Sex role reversal is no longer regarded as strange. Appealing to liberated women makes good business sense since they are generally part of the upper middle class, and they and their husbands or roommates are ideal consumers.

Although benign and constructive in several respects, women's liberation is fundamentally antagonistic to the working class because it is an attack on family life itself. The ethos of this sort of feminism is hostile to the institution of lifelong marriage, to the concept of wife as homemaker, and to the proposition that raising children full-time is an honorable calling. The ethos of the working class is quite the opposite: "the deep family orientation of the working class is perhaps its principal characteristic,"[25] and the values of marriage and parenthood still find "their clearest and liveliest expression in the white working class."[26]

Contrary to the ideology of women's liberation, working-class women do not regard homemaking as degrading, as a gilded form of slavery. One of the primary grievances working-class women have against the women's liberation movement is this denigration of the homemaker. Lillian Breslow Rubin, a women's liberationist, quotes one such woman as saying, "They put you down if you want to be married and raise kids, like there's something the matter with you."[27]

The notion that there is something odious about homemaking was not a 1960s invention; it has been a notion common to college-educated upper-middle-class women for decades. Such women, who have always made a sharp distinction between the blessedness of brain work and the cursedness of manual work, are prone to feel that they are "too good for housework."[28]

Now that these women are entering the work force en masse, they naturally gravitate toward high-paying, classy careers. No wonder working-class women are alienated from women's liberation. They are not comfortable with the concept that manual labor is beneath contempt; they are under no illusion that they are too good for housework. Hence, they perceive the liberationist attack on homemaking as an attack on *them*.

Women's liberationists, who extol capitalism's world of work at the expense of work in the home, look to the world of upper-middle-class occupations as their lodestar. As such, women's liberation is grounded in old bourgeois prejudices.

Recently at Bryn Mawr, a swishy Eastern women's college, a popular tee shirt proclaimed, "Our failures only marry."[29] The obvious message was that traditional marriage is a dismal state and a mark of downward mobility and that the purpose of a Bryn Mawr education is to put women into the labor force—not as waitresses or welders but as professionals and businesswomen. Instead of just qualifying a woman to marry a banker, which is what a Bryn Mawr education used to do for a woman, now the point is to become a banker. What the Bryn Mawr tee shirts proclaimed is that women who "only" marry are failures—the flotsam and jetsam of womanhood. The arrogance is blinding, as is that of the needlepoint sign offered in numerous mail-order catalogues that declares: "Dull Women Have Immaculate Homes."

The liberationist put-down of homemaking because it doesn't earn "real" money is indicative of the bourgeois-materialist thrust of women's liberation, which reduces the marital relationship to a cash relationship. It measures everything in terms of cash or market value. A recent theme is that husbands ought to pay housewives a "real" wage for what they do, with payments to the Social Security Administration included. If you don't get paid for doing something, it's not worth doing. Your worth as a human being, then, is directly proportional to your income, according to this line of reasoning.

ABORTION AND SELF-INTEREST

As noted above, the women's movement was born out of the upper-middle-class student movement of the 1960s. The rise of women's liberation in the radical movement was another indication of the profound shift in the tenor of the radicalism of the 1960s from social idealism to personal aggrandizement. Several radical organizations were fractured by the rise of radical feminism and proceeded to collapse. Radical feminists came to regard their personal liberation as of greater importance than the class liberation that radical organizations were ostensibly trying to effect. Jane Alpert, an Adam Smith of radical feminism, summed up the mood when she urged her sisters to "let your own self-interest be your highest priority."[30]

True to this imperative, not only organizations were wrecked but so were marriages and families. Children, now perceived as nuisances and shackles, were deprived of fathers and packed off to day-care centers or handed over to the divorced husbands for custody so that the women could maximize their self-interest. Have men treated women as inferior objects? These women would see to it that that ended, even if it meant treating their own children as inferior objects, even if it meant killing the flesh of their flesh in their own wombs.

One of the major triumphs of the women's movement has been the legalization of abortion. Abortion is antifamily in ethos and effect, for it is most often resorted to by sexually active unmarried females who are seeking to prevent or postpone the launching of a family. But abortion is also attractive to married members of the upper middle class. Business and professional people are career people, and children and family chores constitute handicaps in the bourgeoisie's "great achievement race."

Careerists do meaningful work with which the satisfactions of family life allegedly cannot compare. But to the average man, who is not terribly mobile either occupationally or geographically, family and children are welcome refuges from a dull, exhausting, and cold environment. They are sources of suffering but also of incomparable love and warmth, which explains why poorer people have larger families than richer people. The commoner finds his meaning in his family, the traditional organic (not individualistic) family. Just as the greatest resistance to permissive child rearing, women's liberation, and unisex is found in the working class, so is the greatest resistance to abortion found there.

The passion for legal abortion is thoroughly bourgeois, deriving in most instances from materialistic egotism grounded in veiled appeals to property rights. Children get in the way of fun, careers, and self-fulfillment. Children are like crabgrass growing in one's private garden. Ti-Grace Atkinson, the daughter of an upper-middle-class Louisiana family and another Adam Smith of radical feminism, has justified abortion on the grounds that a woman's reproductive organs are her private property.[31] No crabgrass in the womb, if you please. That sounds gross, of course, so the current euphemism is that "a woman has the right to control her own body." As if there were no other body—that of the unborn child—involved. As if unborn children—half of whom are female—have no right to control *their* own bodies.

Thanks to the U.S. Supreme Court, the unborn child is at the mercy of the self-interest of the pregnant mother. The father has no say about whether the mother of their child may have an abortion, and in most cases a girl under age eighteen need not have parental consent to have an abortion. This is the spirit of individualism, dividing the wife from the husband and the girl from her parents. It is a dagger aimed at the heart of working-class values, not to mention Christian values.

"WE" ARE "THEY"

Most Christians understand the anti-Christian character of abortion, of sexual liberation, and much of feminism. But we need to consider how our own desires for upward mobility, and our success in achieving it, put us in a situation where we come face to face with the very conditions that nurtured the cultural revolution in the first place: affluence, sophistication, free time, lots of options, preoccupation with self, and so forth.

When we move up in society, we may not only leave behind old friends, but we may also experience intense pressures to leave behind older, more frugal, more self-restrained habits and values. But if we are to continue to uphold those traditional values, we should maintain our friendships with those old friends who are advocates of such values.

When we move up, we may look down on people who haven't moved up with us. We may suddenly think they are unworthy, dull-witted, shortsighted, and perhaps lazy. We forget that from the perspective of Christ on the cross, we are all unworthy. We forget that whatever good things come to us in this life, we dare not claim credit for earning them, for we don't deserve the greatest thing of all: redemption.

As Christians we must appreciate that our lives are permeated with unmerited grace which is "always a step ahead of us, turning our achievements into gifts, our discoveries into revelations, and our choices into the knowledge of being chosen."[32] Unless we confess our total dependence on God's grace, we fall right into that most vicious sin of pride, which was the original sin of Adam and Eve.

If we let go of our pride and self-satisfaction, we will no longer be able to look down on others as social inferiors. And if we truly come to appreciate the signs of grace among the common people, particularly their strong devotion to traditional family values, we will discover that we have no basis for feeling proud and self-satisfied.

The artificial barriers between "us" and "them" will dissolve. Indeed, if we consider our own roots, we will sooner or later realize that "we" *are* "they." All of us, however noble a pedigree we may claim, will find that at some point we sprang from common workers or peasants, just like everyone else. We gain nothing by trying to pretend that we are special.

131

And if we trace our family trees all the way back, we will all see that we are direct descendants of that first couple fleeing the garden under the judgment of the Lord God. If we are to boast, then, let us boast with Paul of our weaknesses (see 2 Cor. 11:30; 12:5 NEB).

SEX AND CLASS

Christians troubled by the sexual revolution need to realize that that revolution has a "class" character, and it is not exclusively about sex. Fundamentally, it is about selfishness, and the solution begins within our own selves. By understanding the bourgeois character of the sexual revolution, and the bourgeois aspirations in our own hearts, we better realize that we can get all fired up about sexual perversion and yet be in spiritual danger. It is easy to speak out for clean living, all the while being "greedy of filthy lucre" (1 Tim. 3:3) and scrambling to make it to the top.

The problem of greed is not just a matter of good works. Greed is a matter of the heart, of our faith, as when Paul said, "No. . . covetous man, who is an idolater, hath any inheritance in the kingdom of Christ and of God" (Eph. 5:5). The greedy man makes for himself idols that he reveres and trusts more than God. Idolatry is literally a form of faithlessness, and to stop believing is to jeopardize one's salvation.

Yet, it is so natural to want to worship *both* God and mammon. Given the success-oriented society we live in and take for granted, we easily fall into the assumption that, as Jerry Falwell has said, "Jesus likes winners."

When we value success, we also value the very structure and ideology of success, and we find we no longer have time for the poor and needy, for the "losers." We are incapable, then, of obeying Paul's admonition to "mind not high things, but condescend to men of low estate" (Rom. 12:16).

SEEKING OUT THE LOWLY

In our understandable preoccupation with the sexual revolution, we Christians forget that lust is only one of the seven deadly sins. When we join the upper-middle-class's great achievement race, we make ourselves particularly vulnerable to four other deadly sins: pride, covetousness, envy, and gluttony.

We need to pay close attention to our own class ambitions if we are to be armed against these four other sins. And we must cultivate the corresponding virtues of humility, generosity, compassion, and simplicity. A mystique of poverty pervades church history, and that is why Mother Teresa tells her audiences that they must not only help the poor, they must also honor the poor, get to know the poor, and identify with the poor.

It is spiritually salutary to be able to identify with the poor or, more realistically and modestly, with common people in our own country. For if we are able to identify with those of low estate, we will likely be less absorbed with our own pride, covetousness, envy, and gluttony. We need to realize that there is a social component to Christian virtue. If we are going to be serious about humility, generosity, compassion, and simplicity, we may have to give up our hopes for upward mobility and even be willing to risk a little downward mobility.

As Henri Nouwen points out, "the story of our salvation stands radically over and against the philosophy of upward mobility." The Incarnation is the biggest put-down in cosmic history. God became man—and a man of humble circumstances at that. Jesus did not achieve anything for Himself, and He died a seeming failure on the cross. People had wanted to make Him an earthly king, but His only crown was a crown of thorns, not self-esteem. As Nouwen puts it, "the whole life of Jesus of Nazareth was a life in which all upward mobility was resisted."[33]

If we are to be true followers of Christ, we too must eschew the worldly crown, and to do that entails a willingness to orient ourselves toward the less fortunate rather than the distorted values of many of the more fortunate. Robert Coles, who has lived with and studied poor people and their children throughout the world over the last twenty years, has noted that Christ's life is "a constant source of inspiration to this century's poor. They attend His words. They regard closely His manner of living. They do not overlook the company He kept...ordinary working people."[34]

God's way is to seek out the lowly. As Paul taught, "God hath chosen the foolish things of the world to confound the wise; and God hath chosen the weak things of the world to confound the things which are mighty; and base things of the world, and things which are despised, hath God chosen" (1 Cor. 1:27-28). It is not surprising that "not many wise men after the flesh, not many mighty, not many noble, are called" (1 Cor. 1:26).

The way of Jesus is not the way of riches, cleverness, fame, and power. He teaches that He meets us not at the pinnacle of success but in the guise of the lowly: "Verily I say unto you, Inasmuch as ye have done it unto one of the least of these my brethren, ye have done it unto me" (Matt. 25:40).

THE GOSPEL AND THE POOR

The Bible teaches that God loves all men but that He holds a preference for the care of the poor. Jesus identified only one group as the special recipients of His gospel, namely, the poor. For example, quoting Isaiah in the synagogue, He said, "The Spirit of the Lord is upon me, because he hath anointed me to preach the gospel to the poor" (Luke 4:18), adding that these words were fulfilled in Himself (see Luke 4:21). Not surprisingly, Jesus spent most of His time with the poor in the countryside of Galilee, not with the powerful and wealthy in Jerusalem.

Indeed, that He concerned Himself primarily with the poor and unfortunate was a sign of His messiahship. John the Baptist sent two messengers to Jesus to find out if He was the long-awaited Messiah. Jesus answered by pointing to His deeds: "The blind receive their sight, and the lame walk, the lepers are cleansed, and the deaf hear, the dead are raised up, and the poor have the gospel preached to them" (Matt. 11:5). Therefore, that most of the disciples chosen by Jesus were fishermen and other common people is understandable.

Indeed, James berated his fellow Christians for showing a preference for the rich:

For if there come unto your assembly a man with a gold ring, in goodly apparel, and there come in also a poor man in vile raiment...ye have respect to him that weareth the gay clothing, and say unto him, sit thou here in a good place; and say to the poor, stand thou there, or sit here under my footstool.

This is "evil," said James, because God has "chosen the poor of this world [to be] rich in faith, and heirs of the kingdom" (James 2:2-5).

Jesus instructs us to show partiality toward the poor in such a trivial thing as the guests we invite to dinner: "When thou makest a dinner...call not thy...rich neighbors....But...call the poor, the maimed, the lame, the blind" (Luke 14:12-13). The same applies to lending (see Luke 6:34-35).[35]

We can express our solidarity with common people only if we reorient our personal values away from the lifestyle of the successful. Otherwise, we will have, as the secular world is constantly urging us to have, a preferential love not for the poor but for the standards of achievement of so many of the successful.

This is not to say we must sport a false humility, exhibit a conspicuous proletarianism, or eschew excellence in whatever the Lord has called us to do with our lives. But in our lives and occupations, we must not let our quest for excellence be confused with a bald quest for success, or distract us from God, our families, or the needy. This is the Christian way out of the trap of self-indulgence.

REGAINING MORAL
AND SOCIAL VISION

The family...helps to keep alive an alternative to the values which dominate the marketplace. •
Jean Bethke Elshtain

Marxism, which purports to speak for the lowly, is actually, according to Erazim Kohák, a "grand illusion—and leaves behind the need for a grand, not a mundane truth."[1] Both Communism and, to a much lesser extent, Western socialism are descendants of Marxism, and both lack the moral and spiritual vision that is the difference between a grand illusion and a grand truth. If socialism has severed its links to the family-minded moral intuition of common people, and if Communism is a betrayal of common people by Party bureaucrats, where can we turn for inspiration?

The most compelling partisanship on behalf of common people and family morality has historically come from orthodox Christians, many of them Roman Catholics. Their partisanship has a spiritual and ascetic depth that is abidingly and generically radical.

137

THE GRAND TRUTH

Orthodox Christianity provides that needed grand truth mentioned by Kohák. Its vision of the new age—of a new heaven and a new earth where the last shall be first—transcends anything Marxism can envision.

Furthermore, unlike Marxism, the church is able to appropriate some of the new age in the lives of people in the present. Marxism simply has no way of matching all the St. Francises of Assisi, Dorothy Days, and Mother Teresas that Christendom perennially produces, people who live out an option for the poor, day in and day out. The words and good deeds of these exemplars—and others such as Bonhoeffer, Wilberforce, and Padre Pio—touch the lives of countless people throughout the world.

It is a misconception to think the Christian faith entails giving up all hope for this world. As the Second Vatican Council so poignantly put it,

> while we are warned that it profits a man nothing if he gain the whole world and lose himself, the expectation of a new earth must not weaken but rather stimulate our concern for cultivating this one. For here grows the body of a new human family, a body which even now is able to give some kind of foreshadowing of the new age (*Gaudium et Spes*, par. 39).

That our actions can have some mysterious foreshadowing relationship to the kingdom of God elevates them above and beyond the mundane measurements of the gross national product, against which the successes of capitalism, socialism, and Communism are conventionally measured.

Christianity's emphasis on the absoluteness of right and wrong, on doing good for its own sake rather than for utilitarian reasons, on the integrity of the family, and on the priority of giving over receiving (for it is "in giving that we receive," as St. Francis said) would provide the political Left with the moral vision it lacks. The ability of individuals to transcend self-interest is indestructibly rooted not in secular humanism but in the conviction that in dying we are born to a new life.

Catholic social teaching has developed a class perspective, recovering a perspective already present in Scripture. According to the 1971 Synod of Bishops, "In the Old Testament God reveals himself to us as the liberator of the oppressed and the defender of the poor." Christ proclaimed "the intervention of God's justice on behalf of the needy and the oppressed (Luke 6:21-23). In this way he identified himself with his 'least brethren.' "[2]

That the poor are given theological preference in the Scriptures potentially gives Christians a more abiding class perspective than either Western socialism, which is usually content to manage existing class-ridden capitalist economies, or Communism, which in fact transfers its theoretical preference for the working class from actual workers to an elite of Party professionals.

As Christians, we know that there will never be a perfect, classless society before the Second Coming. Regardless of how just or fair any society is, it will always have within it those who are (at least relatively) poor, weak, powerless, sick, or otherwise deprived. Sadly, secular messianic ideologies are quite unprepared for such a situation. Even "after the revolution," there will need to be people who continue to side with the weak, who challenge the pride and insensitivity of the strong.

In a postrevolutionary society where everyone is getting more affluent, there will always be a need for people who alert society to the shallowness and ugliness of greed and self-indulgence, who recall people to the gospel virtues of simplicity, poverty of spirit, and modesty of ambition. Long after triumphant socialists or Communists have grown smug and lazy, therefore, Christians will surely be tending to the needs of "the least of these my brethren."

FAMILY PLAN

Meanwhile, Western socialists should be aware of how bizarre it is for them to pillory the family as a "bourgeois" institution. Family life is hardly limited to the upper middle class, and the organic family is an inescapably collectivist institution. The family is uniquely a place where rewards are primarily distributed according to need, not work or merit or luck, and where the harsh judgments of the marketplace can be neutralized by love and forgiveness. Hence, the family is the embyro of a less abrasive, less calculating society, and it constitutes an uncertain friend of that highly competitive style of capitalism where the needy can be ignored and where only the "fit" deserve to survive.

The old socialist slogans—"production for use, not profit," "cooperation before competition," and "the common good over the private good"—apply directly to the structure and mystique of the family. The family is a veritable paradigm of socialism, as even the East Germans and Soviets realize. Even Marxist slogans apply. Ideally, the family should function according to the Communist principle of "from each according to his ability, to each according to his need."

To share one's worldly goods and to sacrifice one's personal comfort and convenience to the needs of loved ones require a socialist spirit in all of us. What socialism has failed to incarnate in societies, the family has achieved day after day throughout the world. Socialism at its best is simply the extension of the family spirit to the entire society.

If leftists object that devotion to family can interfere with regard for society, they must admit that most people are naturally more concerned with members of their own family than with non-family members—just as individuals are naturally more interested in their own welfare than in that of other individuals, even family members.

Few people can authentically deny self and family on behalf of humanity. The celibate priesthood and monasticism are not exactly popular ways of life.

But for most people most of the time, concern for others will be a result of extending, not negating, the virtues and habits acquired in the family. Liberation from family does not normally liberate one's love of humanity; it only lets the monster of devouring self-love out of its cage. This has been the experience of countless antifamily communes and utopian experiments, as well as of those few Communist countries that initially tried to dismember the family.

On the other hand, the very demanding ideal of sex only within heterosexual marriage, based on a commitment to love one another for life and to generate and provide for new life, has a wondrous way of deflating self-indulgent fantasies. Indeed, it requires ongoing self-discipline. Marital fidelity itself teaches us how to subordinate our desires and interests to a greater good, which makes the traditional family a training camp for building a society that would place common interests ahead of self-interest.

In contrast to family-minded idealism, realism dictates doing whatever impulse commands, whatever involves the least effort. Accept self-interest as a given and go from there. On a personal level, the realistic thing, the easiest thing, to do is live only for oneself: go out and "swing," "cat around"—call it what you will—but above all, maximize immediate personal pleasure without entering into any binding commitments.

The rise of the abortion clinic makes this approach to life very practical. Is this not a modern form of rugged individualism and ruthless competitiveness? "All's fair in love and war," says the old maxim.

It's strange that in regard to family matters, idealistic progressives and radicals usually throw in the towel and become archrealists, while on economic and foreign policy issues, their idealism hardly knows limits. Equally strange is the conservatives' crass realism on economic and foreign policy issues, which coexists with a scintillating idealism on family issues.

CRACKS IN THE CEMENT?

If the socialist ideal can be understood as an extension of the family spirit to society, the cultural revolution represents the extension of the self-centered spirit of capitalism to the family and personal relationships. A few American socialists are beginning to glimpse this, as the hollowness of the liberation mania becomes more self-evident.

Literary critic Irving Howe, bewildered and depressed by the hawking of pornography in the streets of New York City, finds pornography "more destructive of my morale as a socialist" than all the conservative polemics of the previous thirty years.[3] The historian Christopher Lasch, another socialist, sees the cultural revolution as an "invasion of the family by the marketplace and the street...and the perversion of the most intimate relationships by the calculating, manipulative spirit that has long been ascendant in business life."[4]

Even feminists are thinking the unthinkable. At a feminist conference in New York City in 1979 honoring the thirtieth anniversary of Simone de Beauvoir's *The Second Sex*, feminists were heard troubling over "the fact that feminism seems to have flourished only in capitalist countries." They were asking, "Is 'independence' necessarily good, or is this merely part of the atomization and 'me-firstism' of our current cultural life?"[5]

Jane Fonda, a veritable symbol of the American

Left, has said that she has committed herself to remain married to her husband, Tom Hayden, for life. Throwing trendiness to the winds (finally!), she said:

> It would be indulgent for us to allow something to happen to our marriage....It's important as an example to other people. When two people share a vision and have a sense of responsibility beyond themselves, it's important that their marriage work out....You have to have a stable personal life. I don't think you can work to achieve social justice ...without sustenance and support—and children— who are the future.[6]

Only a few American leftists see the connection between capitalism and cultural liberation, and only a few conservatives seem to see it too. The 1980 and 1984 Reagan-Republican platforms, for example, were paeans to both traditional cultural values and the *un*traditional invention called capitalism. Precious few conservatives were able to see any contradiction. But George F. Will did when he complained that

> Republicans see no connection between the cultural phenomena they deplore and the capitalist culture they promise to intensify; no connection between the multiplying evidence of self-indulgence and national decadence...and the unsleeping pursuit of evermore immediate, intense, and grand material gratifications.[7]

It is puzzling that the majority of cultural conservatives continue to cling tenaciously to the capitalism-no-matter-what ideology. Do they really believe modern consumerist capitalism will ever

144

say anything about homosexual bath houses, rent-a-boy, hookers' balls, male striptease for women, women's cosmetics packaged in phalluses—beyond the tattered nostrum about consenting adults, that is?

If leftists are hypocritical about virtue, so are conservatives. Antigovernment conservatives, who want to get government out of people's lives, quickly violate the foundations of their own ideology in the area of personal morality. Here they discover the virtues of what they would otherwise denigrate as big government, somehow forgetting that the decline in personal morality can be traced in part to the decline in government interference in this area. They want big government to prohibit a woman from contracting with a doctor for an abortion, to outlaw the commerce in pornography, to crack down on homosexuality and the prostitution traffic, even to write prayers for use in public schools. It is scandalous that conservatives yearn for the public enforcement of personal morality but strenuously avoid speaking prophetically on the morals of the economic marketplace.

Take the case of abortion. The 1980 Republican and 1984 platforms called for a constitutional amendment outlawing abortion nationwide. Conservatives never seemed to consider that they were proposing vigorous federal action against the lucrative abortion business, estimated to be a $400-to-$500-million-a-year industry.[8] Conservatives, who are famous for denouncing anyone who would legislate morality or collectivize virtue, were willing to do those very same things. Those who habitually rail and rage against "the feds" fell silent.

The free market has no social sense of "the good." To be a conservative today is to defer to the market. In regard to abortion, this means deferring to the doctor (entrepreneur) and the woman (customer). The market is value free; it posits no vision of the good beyond itself. All it offers is "freedom of choice," which is the proabortionist's bromide. Moreover, to defer to the market is to glorify the individual, which is to disregard Original Sin. Such deference assumes that individuals will act morally and that the common good will automatically be realized when individuals are left to pursue their own self-interest. Just as a Marxist utopianism assumes the collective can always be trusted to act correctly, so too a conservative utopianism assumes the individual can always be trusted to do the right thing.

Hence, conservatives chronically complain about federal regulations protecting consumers, insuring occupational health and safety, guarding the environment, and so forth. But if they can see that the mother cannot always be trusted to do right by her own unborn child, then logically they should also be able to see that the entrepreneur cannot always be trusted to do right by the consumer, his workers, or the environment.

Ironically, the logic of fighting against legalized abortion has implications that are anything but conservative, for not only do antiabortion conservatives inadvertently accept the logic of government regulation they otherwise despise, but they do so—however unconsciously—in the name of a venerable leftist value: human equality. Just as the radical abolitionists of the Civil War era repudiated the notion that the humanity of the Negro was unequal to the humanity of the Caucasian, so do antiabortion conservatives insist that the humanity of the unborn child is equal to that of the full-grown adult.

The logic of free markets and individual freedom has validated the very hedonism most conservatives repudiate. Not only is it a short hop from laissez-faire economics to do-your-own-thing permissiveness, but the freedom conservatives extol is a two-edged sword: the champions of free love habitually emblazon freedom on their banners, as when Planned Parenthood purchased a full-page ad in the February 2, 1981, issue of *Time* magazine noting that the prolife movement's threat to a woman's right to an abortion is a threat to freedom itself. The ad concluded patriotically in bold print: "THE TIME HAS COME AGAIN WHEN AMERICANS MUST FIGHT FOR THEIR FREEDOM."

The current political debate between Left and Right in America is grounded in illogic, even hypocrisy. The time is ripe for the Left to face the fact that its support of the cultural revolution actually reinforces the capitalist ethos it loathes and for the Right to admit that its support of the capitalist ethos fuels the liberationist program it deplores.

Both leftists and rightists need to repent of their self-interested attitudes. Joining them at the altar must be the rest of us, who may feel we are correct on the questions mentioned here, but who certainly fall short of the glory of God in numerous other areas of life. May God have mercy on us all, that we regain our moral and social vision and turn with all our hearts to the righteousness of the kingdom!

BEING A CHRISTIAN
IN A CONSUMER PARADISE

We always find that those who walked closest to
Christ Our Lord were those who had to bear the
greatest trials. • *St. Teresa of Avila*

To recall Mario Savio's words cited earlier, our
society is a "consumer's paradise" that is "simply
no longer exciting." The life of self-indulgence, the
bourgeois life, the life measured out with coffee
spoons, to borrow an image from T. S. Eliot, is indeed a bore.

To a certain extent, the bohemian's critique of
Babbittry is on target. But "excitingness," which
the bohemian counterposes to old-fashioned bourgeois boredom, is hardly a criterion of either the
good society or the fulfilled individual. The bohemian's solution eventually becomes part of the
problem. Indeed, because the solution strips away
the mitigating inhibitions and hypocrisies of old-
fashioned bourgeois life, it makes the problem
even more vicious. Hypocrisy is a tribute that vice
pays to virtue. For, while the life measured out in
spoons of cocaine may be exciting for a while, it
too ultimately ends in boredom—a boredom from
which there may be no escape.

Magnifying the quest for personal pleasure can be heady at first, but since personal pleasure is the guiding principle of the bourgeois way in the first place, one never gets out of the bourgeois rut. One just gets in deeper.

Political radicalism is more promising. As with just about any kind of extreme belief, it is an obvious alternative to a listless, inauthentic life. For example, the Communist movement offers purpose, a sense of the heroic, a life of sacrifice that reaches beyond momentary personal thrills. Moreover, it demands discipline. Yet, its ultimate objective is, rather ironically, the selfsame affluent society, but with the goods, services, and thrills more equally distributed. So, Communism, especially the more it spreads and comes to realization, can be seen to offer no alternative after all. The more affluent Communist societies become, the more difficult it is for them to fend off the lure of moral permissiveness.

Philosophically, Communism does not offer an option to the sated life, but classical fascism did. Mussolini, for one, insisted that the purpose of life is not pleasure but duty. He promised not a static utopia but a life of action, struggle, and self-abnegation.

One of the seminal theorists of struggle was Mussolini's alleged mentor, Georges Sorel. To Sorel, a life of ease was inherently selfish, ethically base, and esthetically disgusting. The antidote was a life of collective struggle, a life punctuated with obstacles and challenges. Properly orchestrated, such a life induces people to forget their private appetites and petty concerns and to reverse the slide into decadence. Confronted by a frightful and hated enemy—and Sorel was not particular about who the enemy should be—people would create community and pull together in common effort. If people would learn how to hate, they would also learn how to love, for, even as Reinhold Niebuhr taught, collective vices can be the foundations of personal virtue.

Truly, there was something ennobling about the dramatic sit-in demonstrations of the 1960s, when people locked arms and destinies and committed themselves to struggle against the military or the white racists or whomever, despite the risks, dangers, and costs. Rather perversely, but similarly, the fascists glorified war because they saw it as the ultimate theater of struggle and sacrifice. They believed, in however warped a way, that there is no greater love than that a man be prepared to lay down his life for his brother.

The tragedy of such teaching is that to keep the sense of the heroic from slackening, ever-new struggles must be devised by the leadership elite, and countless people are bound to get maimed or killed in the process. Sacrifice in the service of contrived, meaningless struggles is absurd. For these and other reasons, fascistic and militaristic philosophies offer no adequate answer to the sated life.

Neither do Western socialism or progressivism offer a solution to our cultural crisis. They only hold out the prospect of gradually equalizing our decadence, something Communism promises to achieve in a more distant future but in a more dramatic way.

For most people most of the time, it seems that self-discipline is an involuntary condition brought on by temporary conditions of adversity. That the working class—which socialism and progressivism claim to champion—seems more virtuous than the upper middle class is not necessarily due to some sort of original innocence enjoyed by the working class. By fortuitous circumstance, its economic resources and cultural sensibility may simply restrict its capacity for self-indulgence and hence envigorate its ethos.

Socialism and progressivism appear unable to foster the spirit of self-discipline outside involuntary conditions of adversity experienced by common people. A socialism or progressivism infused with a sense of the inherent beauty of self-sacrifice and collective endeavor is nowhere on the horizon of the West. Moreover, the reflexive secularism and visceral materialism dominant in socialist and progressive movements virtually destroy such possibilities.

THE REAL SOLUTION

The only manageable and durable solution to decadence is, as I began to learn in East Germany, authentic Christian faith. Jesus Christ our Lord mandates the heroic life of self-discipline and sacrifice as virtual ends in themselves because they are congruent with the only unqualified ends in themselves, namely, God and His will. Indeed, Paul listed "self-control" as one of the gifts of the Spirit (see Gal. 5:23 NASB)!

Unlike the surrogate religions of fascism and Marxism, Christian faith locates the enemy not as the other person, not as another nation, race, or class, but primarily as one's own sin. The Chris-

151

tian monk is called a "soldier of Christ" because he does daily battle with the temptations of his own soul—in short, with the sin that dwells within him.

This struggle for sanctity is never meaningless. It reveals the meaning of life, of both this world and the next. As the writer Georges Bernanos said, the only true adventure is the adventure of sanctity, and as St. Catherine of Siena noted, all the way to heaven *is* heaven because Jesus said, "I am the way."

The danger of politics—any kind of politics—is that it encourages the externalization or impersonalization of the struggle between good and evil, a struggle that is social but also inescapably personal. The struggle against the other person too easily issues forth in hatred. But the struggle against one's own egocentrism can flower into love of neighbor. Religious passion can be the moral equivalent of political passion but also a passion that elevates politics to a level more consonant with the inherent dignity of all human persons. It is a dignity secured by the Incarnation, which disclosed (contrary to all forms of Gnosticism) that men are not so void of worth that God could not appear among them in the flesh. From a Christian perspective, then, political enemies can rarely, if ever, be equated with *the* enemy.

FORSAKING POWER

Earlier, I quoted the East German Protestant bishop D. Moritz Mitzenheim as telling me that East German Christians are not called to rule but to serve. To anyone familiar with the New Testament, this statement should come as no great revelation. But after some fifteen hundred years of Western "Christian" civilization where Christians have indeed ruled, sometimes with kindness, sometimes with indifference, sometimes with brutality, his words can come as a shock. It is not exactly what most Christians want to hear, for it goes against our human nature to let go of our will to power and privilege.

I didn't ask the kindly bishop whether American and West German Christians are also called to forsake power and to serve. But I had to conclude that the great spiritual strength of the East German Christians comes precisely from the fact that they cannot rule and have no choice but to serve.

It is a sad commentary that, on the whole, Christians do not voluntarily forsake power in favor of service (we would rather rationalize our power seeking as an opportunity to serve), but must be forced to do so by alien, hostile forces. I am not claiming that Communism is God's judgment on the faithlessness of Western Christians. I have no way of knowing that, for I am no prophet. But I do know from Scripture and experience that God often visits adversity upon His children in order to make them more faithful servants. That is why we need to pay close attention to our Christian brethren in the East, not only to protest their persecution and lack of human rights, which indeed we must do, but also to be attentive to what God is doing in their lives.

Adversity goes against our grain. Just as we like to be in control of our own lives, so we feel more comfortable in a society where "our kind of people" are in control, where Christianity defines what society regards as right and wrong. But such a social order has been fading steadily since the Enlightenment.

BEYOND FOLK RELIGION

One of the fruits of the Enlightenment has been the separation of church and state—a legal reality in the United States, Eastern Europe, and most of the rest of what used to be called "the Christian world."

With the rise of scientific rationalism and freedom of thought, separation of church and state has tended to slide into the isolation of religion from society. Once the state no longer upholds the institution of the church, it isn't too long before pressure builds up for the state to cease upholding distinctly Christian personal values, values that are largely exclusive to Christians.

Now, in the United States and Western Europe, while there are some minor skirmishes in the area of church-state relations, the major battles are fought in the arena of cultural policy. The burning questions are whether the state should or should not penalize homosexual practice, clean up pornography and prostitution, outlaw abortion, legalize marijuana, and such.

In the United States, Christianity, though not the established religion, is nevertheless the folk religion. I was repelled by that folk religion and had to go all the way to East Germany—where there is neither a state church nor a folk religion, but only a believers' church—in order to find Christ. My conviction has been that, ironically, the church is actually healthier in East Germany than in the

United States, despite superficial appearances to the contrary.

SANCTIFYING OUR MOTIVES

What are we to do about the moral vacuum produced by the cultural revolution in America? There is, I think, a good reason to fight against it; there is also a bad, defective reason to do so. Given the polarization that now affects cultural issues, it is high time that such a distinction be made, for as T. S. Eliot insisted, the greatest treason is to do the right thing for the wrong reason.

The wrong reason for fighting the cultural revolution is that life was so much more pleasant, more predictable, and less challenging before it occurred. This pragmatic reasoning is often linked, sometimes subconsciously, with certain assumptions of our folk religion. One assumption is that the United States was founded as a Christian nation, a historically dubious propositon the founding fathers would deny. Another assumption is similar to it: the United States is God's chosen land, the New Israel (a notion found nowhere in the Bible or Christian tradition). Accordingly, it is not only more pleasant when Christian values predominate, it is supposedly divinely ordained.

In order to guarantee this state of affairs, committed Christians are supposed to get the right people into government and pass the right laws. If we don't do this, it is often said, God will punish the United States, and we will no longer be the greatest nation on the face of the earth (as if power and prosperity are equivalents of blessings, as if good behavior automatically produces such blessings). Whether the assumptions here are pragmatic or folk-religious or both, they are self-serving, modernistic inventions of man's mind and alien to orthodox, apostolic Christianity.

I grant that for the Christian, life is indeed more pleasant when Christian values predominate. It is always comforting when our values are reaffirmed by society and enforced by the state. But we must remember that Christ did *not* promise us a pleasant and comfortable life without worries, challenges, or frightening problems. If we want Christian values to be supreme because we feel entitled to have things just the way we want them, then maybe it's better for us if Christian values are *not* written into the law of the land. For the surest way for Christians to become smug, lazy, and flabby is for us to live in a milieu where everything can be taken for granted, where everything is secure, where we walk by sight and not by faith.

When the church is esteemed by the world, worldly values often come to be esteemed by the church. When Christians seem to be ruling, the church becomes respectable, social climbers enter her doors for reasons of personal advancement, and the ambitious find the ordained ministry an attractive career option. Weighed down with deadwood, the church too easily becomes a function of society and a captive to the world. She becomes not a servant church—not even a ruling church—but actually a subservient church.

The right reason for fighting the cultural revolution has nothing to do with folk religion or with the status anxiety Christians suffer in seeing their values eroded and mocked. We are not called to work against being stigmatized for being differ-

156

ent. We should expect to see our social standing in the world imperiled, at least on occasion. Nor should our resistance to a libertine culture have anything to do with whatever pleasure we might get out of seeing sinners punished. God will take care of that in His own ways and at His own appointed time.

The right reason is simply that Christian values—chastity, marriage, family, fidelity, children, modesty, love for others—are the only values that are true and that bring genuine happiness to people. They bring people nearer to God's will for their lives. A great mystery and paradox of Christianity is that when we give, we receive all the more; when we discipline our own desires and commit ourselves to others, we become truly free; when we forgive, we are forgiven; when we die to our selves, we realize our true selves; and when our lives are over, death is but the gateway to a larger life. Self-fulfillment is not sought for its own sake; it is discovered, often unexpectedly, in the midst of self-denial and self-transcendence.

Obviously, these are deep interior truths of the heart; they cannot be imposed on people for their own good. They cannot be legislated, though good legislation can circumscribe some of the grosser forms of self-absorption. Christians are not earthly utopians, and we cannot expect miracles from politics. Nevertheless, we should resist the cultural revolution in the political arena, as long as our motive is a concern for the well-being, the *true* well-being, of those who, however willingly, participate in that revolution. Our motive must not be a concern for our own convenience or prestige, nor a resentful urge to get back at those who may seem to be having so much fun. This is especially important in the case of abortion, where the very *life* of the unborn should be our greatest concern.

If we can agree that Christians today are not to rule but to serve, we must ask, How are we to serve? We serve by living the gospel so that men might see the light that is within us, by preaching the gospel so that they might be saved, by caring for the needy and less fortunate since faith without works is dead, and by seeking to infuse society with Christian values that bring true peace, joy, and self-fulfillment to others.

COUNTING IT ALL JOY

Voluntary self-denial can be a profoundly and mysteriously Christian passage to greater Christian joy for us, but *in*voluntary occasions of adversity can also provide such a passage for us. St. Angela of Foligna, the thirteenth century mystic, is known for having taught that voluntary suffering is not half as spiritually efficacious as suffering imposed by circumstances and cheerfully endured. Reflecting on self-denial, Dorothy Day said, "Most of us have not the courage to set out on this path wholeheartedly, so God arranges it for us."[1] It would seem that sometimes God arranges adversity—even *social* adversity—for us so that we might, if we are willing, taste His sweetness all the more.

One of the greatest devotional books of all time is *The Imitation of Christ,* dating from the fifteenth century, and thought by many to be the most widely read book in the world other than the

Bible. Thomas à Kempis, the probable author, wrote: "Jesus has now many lovers of His heavenly kingdom, but few that are willing to bear His cross....He finds many companions of His table, but few of His abstinence....Many reverence His miracles, but few follow the ignominy of His cross" (Book Two, Chap. 11, sec. 1). If this was true in the fifteenth century, it is no less true today!

Because we live in a consumer's paradise, we are surfeited with comforts and conditioned to crave even greater comforts. This craving has infected some of our churches and evangelistic activities, whereby Jesus is virtually sold to people on the promise that He will give them wealth, health, popularity, positive self-images, exciting sex lives, obedient children, and what not.

Some sensitive Christians, aghast at the superficiality of a consumer society and a consumer religion, wonder how we might get free of the spiritual paralysis that follows therefrom. Beholding the spiritual depth and vitality of our persecuted brethren in the Communist world and elsewhere, they wonder how we in America might more closely approximate Thomas à Kempis's "Way of the Cross."

And yet, if we consider the way the cultural revolution has devastated Christian culture in this country and made a mockery of those of us who hold fast to Christian morality, we may start to realize that, in a sense, we too are partaking of "the ignominy of His cross." Perhaps God has already arranged it for us.

But there is more to consider. Thomas à Kempis also said that "they that love Jesus for Jesus' sake and not for any comfort of their own, bless Him no less in tribulation and anguish of heart than in the greatest consolation" (Book Two, Chap. 11, sec. 2). Those who love Jesus for Jesus' sake often wind up as saints. The rest of us who so often love Him for our own selfish ends, do so, let us admit it, because we have a high estimation of our own importance, we take ourselves very seriously. But, as the writer G. K. Chesterton observed, "Seriousness is not a virtue....It is really a natural trend or lapse into taking one's self gravely....It is easy to be heavy: hard to be light. Satan fell by the force of gravity." Conversely, "a characteristic of the great saints is their power of levity. Angels can fly because they can take themselves lightly."[2]

As we struggle to restore Christian culture, to alleviate the suffering of our brethren in the East, to identify with the lowly, to bring a greater degree of social justice to this world, and to restrain our own cravings for comfort, let us struggle bravely. But let us not take ourselves and our projects too seriously, too gravely.

And in spite of our own weaknesses, let us not be too afraid to drink of the chalice of Christ's suffering, so that one day we may be able to say to one another, with James, "Consider it all joy...when you encounter various trials; knowing that the testing of your faith produces endurance. And let endurance have its perfect result, that you may be perfect and complete, lacking in nothing" (James 1:2-4 NASB).

Yes, let us count it *all* joy! In doing so, we may find ourselves, at times, *flying*...into the arms of our Lord!

N O T E S

Chapter One

1. William Petersen, "What is Left at Berkeley," in *The Berkeley Student Revolt*, eds. Seymour Martin Lipset and Sheldon S. Wolin (Garden City, N.Y.: Anchor, 1965), p. 370.

2. Jack Weinberg, "The Free Speech Movement and Civil Rights," in *Berkeley Student Revolt*, pp. 221-22.

3. Sheldon S. Wolin and John S. Schaar, "The Abuses of the Multiversity," in *Berkeley Student Revolt*, p. 361.

4. Weinberg, "The Free Speech Movement," p. 224.

5. Mario Savio, "An End to History," in *Berkeley Student Revolt*, p. 219.

6. Mario Savio, "The Future of the Student Movement," speech in Berkeley, Calif., November 20, 1964, quoted in Lewis S. Feuer, *The Conflict of Generations* (New York: Basic Books, 1969), p. 504.

7. Michael Harrington, "The Mystical Militants," in *Thoughts of Young Radicals* (Washington, D.C.: New Republic Books, 1966), p. 67.

8. David Kamen, "Social Styles: The New Left as the New Fraternity," *Daily Californian* [Berkeley student newspaper], November 1, 1966, p. 10.

9. Leslie Woolf Hedley, "The Bohemian New Left— Part II," *The Minority of One* 7 (June 1965): 13.

10. See Sara Davidson, *Loose Change: The Women of the Sixties* (Garden City, N.Y.: Doubleday, 1977), p. 256.

11. Robert Brustein, *Revolution as Theatre* (New York: Liveright, 1971), p. 18.

12. Eugene Genovese, "The Fortunes of the Left," *National Review* 22 (December 1, 1970): 1267.

Chapter Two

1. Eugene Genovese, "Our America" [symposium], *Newsweek* 88 (July 4, 1976): 48.

2. Tom Wolfe, *Radical Chic and Mau-Mauing the Flak Catchers* (New York: Bantam, 1970), pp. 14, 25.

3. Davidson, *Loose Change*, pp. 56-57.

Chapter Three

1. John Warwick Montgomery, "East Side, West Side," *Christianity Today* 18 (March 1, 1974): 112.

2. Karl Barth, *Letters: 1961-1968* (Grand Rapids, Mich.: Eerdmans, 1981), p. 121.

Chapter Four

1. Johannes Hamel, *A Christian in East Germany* (London: SCM Press, 1960), p. 77.

2. Mother Teresa, "The Kiss of Jesus," *New Oxford Review* 49 (December 1982): 4.

3. St. John of the Cross, *Dark Night of the Soul*, 3rd rev. ed. (Garden City, N.Y.: Doubleday Image, 1959), pp. 154-55.

4. Dmitri Dudko, *Our Hope* (Crestwood, N.Y.: St. Vladimir's Seminary Press, 1977), p. 183.

Chapter Five

1. Karol Wojtyla, as quoted in George Huntston Williams, *The Mind of John Paul II* (New York: Seabury, 1981), p. 251.

2. Karl Barth, "Letter to a Pastor in the German Democratic Republic," in Karl Barth and Johannes Hamel, *How to Serve God in a Marxist Land* (New York: Association Press, 1959), pp. 64-65.

3. John Francis Kavanaugh, *Following Christ in a Consumer Society* (Maryknoll, N.Y.: Orbis, 1981), p. 155.

4. Barth, "Letter to a Pastor," p. 65.

Chapter Six

1. Some of the most important evidence upon which the consensus is built can be found in: Kenneth Keniston, *Young Radicals* (New York: Harcourt, Brace & World, 1968); Keniston, *Youth and Dissent* (New York: Harcourt Brace Jovanovich, 1971), pp. 143-68, 303-17; Richard Flacks, "The Liberated Generation: An Exploration of the Roots of Student Protest," *Journal of Social Issues* 23 (July 1967): 52-75; Seymour Martin Lipset, *Rebellion in the University* (Chicago: University of Chicago Press, 1976), chaps. 2, 3. There is virtually no support for the Oedipus complex explanation of student rebellion offered by Feuer's *Conflict of Generations*. The approach is riddled with difficulties—e.g., see Keniston, *Youth and Dissent*, pp. 306-7, and Dale Vree, "A Comment on [Feuer's] 'Some Irrational Sources of Opposition to the Market System,'" in *Capitalism: Sources of Hostility*, ed. Ernest van den Haag (New Rochelle, N.Y.: Epoch Books, 1979), pp. 153-72.

2. Christopher Lasch, *Haven in a Heartless World: The Family Besieged* (New York: Basic Books, 1977), p. 130. For quantitative evidence, see "Opinion Roundup" section, *Public Opinion* 2 (June/July 1979): 33-34, and Daniel Yankelovich, *The New Morality* (New York: Mc-Graw-Hill, 1974).

3. Seymour Martin Lipset and Irving Louis Horowitz, *Dialogues on American Politics* (New York: Oxford University Press, 1978), p. 38.

4. Morris Dickstein, *Gates of Eden: American Culture in the Sixties* (New York: Basic Books, 1977), p. x.

5. Ibid., pp. 71, 81, 82. For concurring views, see Nathan Glazer, "The Role of the Intellectuals," *Commentary* 51 (February 1971): 57-58; Lipset, *Rebellion in the University*, p. xxxi; and Edward Shils, *The Intellectuals and the Powers and Other Essays* (Chicago: University of Chicago Press, 1972), p. 185.

6. John D. Rockefeller 3rd, *The Second American Revolution* (New York: Harper & Row, 1973), pp. 43, 46.

7. "An Elegy for the New Left," *Time* 110 (August 15, 1977): 67; "Milestones," *Time* 111 (May 8, 1978): 82; "Ru-

bin Relents: Now He Promotes Capitalism," *Time* 116 (August 11, 1980): 23; and Jerry Rubin, Letter to the Editor, *Time* 116 (September 22, 1980): E2.

Chapter Seven

1. See Daniel Bell, *The Cultural Contradictions of Capitalism* (New York: Basic Books, 1976), pp. 21-22, 54, 84, and Bell, *The Coming of Post-Industrial Society* (New York: Basic Books, 1973), p. 480. Capitalism has "dug its own grave by the furious promotion of a hedonistic society" [Bell, Letter to the Editor, *The New York Review of Books* 20 (January 24, 1974): 50].

2. Irving Kristol, *Two Cheers for Capitalism* (New York: Basic Books, 1978), pp. 260-61.

3. Bell, *Cultural Contradictions*, p. 21.

4. Paul C. Vitz, *Psychology as Religion: The Cult of Self-Worship* (Grand Rapids, Mich.: Eerdmans, 1977), p. 131.

5. See E. Michael Jones, "Lust and Usury: Two Sides of the Same Coin," *New Oxford Review* 48 (June 1981): 2-3.

6. Brendan Gill, *Here at the New Yorker* (New York: Berkley, 1975), p. 52.

7. Tom Wolfe, *Mauve Gloves & Madmen, Clutter & Vine* (New York: Farrar, Straus and Giroux, 1976), p. 167.

8. Susan Sontag, "Some Thoughts on the Right Way (for us) to Love the Cuban Revolution," *Ramparts* 7 (April 1969): 10.

9. Richard Flacks, "Young Intelligentsia in Revolt," *Trans-action* 7 (June 1970): 55.

10. Bell, *Cultural Contradictions*, p. 37. Also see Kristol, *Two Cheers*, p. 139.

11. Bell, *Post-Industrial Society*, p. 479.

12. Everett C. Ladd, Jr., "Traditional Values Regnant," *Public Opinion* 1 (March/April 1978): 49.

Chapter Eight

1. John Kenneth Galbraith, *The New Industrial State*, rev. and updated (New York: Mentor, 1971), p. 202.

2. Stuart Ewen, *Captains of Consciousness: Advertis-*

ing and the Social Roots of the Consumer Culture (New York: McGraw-Hill, 1976), p. 184. Also see Robert Wuthnow, *The Consciousness Reformation* (Berkeley: University of California Press, 1976), pp. 204-7.

3. James Hitchcock, "The Uses of Tradition," *The Review of Politics* 35 (January 1973): 9.

4. Jim Hougan, *Decadence* (New York: Morrow, 1975), pp. 212-22.

5. Dickstein, *Gates of Eden*, p. 213.

6. George Orwell, *The Road to Wigan Pier* (New York: Berkley, 1961), p. 147.

7. Erazim Kohák, "On the Failure of Marxism," *New Oxford Review* 46 (October 1979): 20.

Chapter Nine

1. See Richard Lemon, *The Troubled American* (New York: Simon and Schuster, 1970), pp. 176, 236.

2. See Louis Harris, *The Anguish of Change* (New York: Norton, 1973), p. 37.

3. See *The Gallup Opinion Index*, no. 60 (June 1970): 22.

4. See William Schneider, "Public Opinion: The Beginning of Ideology?" *Foreign Policy*, no. 17 (Winter 1974-75): 101.

5. See *The Gallup Opinion Index*, no. 178 (June 1980): 16.

6. See *The Gallup Opinion Index*, no. 113 (November 1974): 15.

7. See *The Gallup Opinion Index*, no. 153 (April 1978): 26.

8. See Everett C. Ladd, Jr., "Pursuing the New Class: Social Theory and Survey Data," in *The New Class?*, ed. B. Bruce-Briggs (New Brunswick, N.J.: Transaction Books, 1979), p. 108.

9. See Edward G. Grabb, "Working-Class Authoritarianism and Tolerance of Outgroups: A Reassessment," *The Public Opinion Quarterly* 43 (Spring 1979): 42.

10. Ladd, "Pursuing the New Class" p. 121, 121n.

11. Shirley MacLaine, as interviewed in anon., " 'The People I Love Are Not Conventional,' " *McCall's* 99 (March 1972): 16.

12. See Robert Coles, *The Middle Americans* (Boston: Little, Brown, 1971), p. 13.

13. Lee Rainwater, "Making the Good Life: Working-Class Family and Life-Styles," in *Blue-Collar Workers*, ed. Sar A. Levitan (New York: McGraw-Hill, 1971), p. 209.

14. Herbert Gans, *Popular Culture and High Culture* (New York: Basic Books, 1974), p. 85.

15. Robert Endleman, "Moral Perspectives of Blue-Collar Workers," in *Blue-Collar World*, ed. Arthur B. Shostak and William Gomberg (Englewood Cliffs, N.J.: Prentice-Hall, 1964), p. 313.

16. Lillian Breslow Rubin, *Worlds of Pain: Life in the Working-Class Family* (New York: Basic Books, 1976), p. 126.

17. Edward Banfield, *The Unheavenly City Revisited* (Boston: Little, Brown, 1974), p. 187.

18. See Kenneth A. Feldman and Theodore M. Newcomb, *The Impact of College on Students* (San Francisco: Jossey-Bass, 1969), vol. I: pp. 10, 23-24, 31, 34, 48; and Alexander W. Astin, *Four Critical Years: Effects of College on Beliefs, Attitudes, and Knowledge* (San Francisco: Jossey-Bass, 1977), pp. 60, 78, 80.

19. See Feldman and Newcomb, *Impact of College*, chap. 10. Cf. Astin, *Four Critical Years*, chap. 7.

20. James Q. Wilson, "Liberalism versus Liberal Education," *Commentary* 53 (June 1972): 51.

21. S. M. Miller and Frank Riessman, "The Working Class Subculture," in *Class and Personality in Society*, ed. Alan L. Grey (New York: Atherton, 1969), p. 105.

22. Ibid., p. 110.

23. Richard Flacks, "Who Protests: The Social Bases of the Student Movement," in *Protest!* ed. Julian Foster and Durward Long (New York: Morrow, 1970), p. 151.

24. Frederick Lewis Allen, *Only Yesterday* (New York: Bantam, 1931), p. 129. Also see Ewen, *Captains of Consciousness*, p. 106.

25. Rainwater, "Making the Good Life," p. 209.

26. Rubin, *Worlds of Pain*, p. 68.

27. See ibid., p. 130.

28. Mirra Komarovsky, *Blue-Collar Marriage* (New

York: Vintage, 1967), p. 57.

29. See Ellen Wilson, "The Ineluctable Happy Ending," *The Human Life Review* 4 (Spring 1978): 33.

30. Jane Alpert, quoted in Edward E. Ericson, Jr., *Radicals in the University* (Stanford, Calif.: Hoover Institution Press, 1975), p. 50.

31. See Ti-Grace Atkinson, *Amazon Odyssey* (New York: Links Books, 1974), pp. 1-3.

32. Richard John Neuhaus, "Law and the Rightness (and Wrongness) of Things," *Worldview* 22 (September 1979): 41.

33. Henri Nouwen, "The Selfless Way of Christ," *Sojourners* 10 (June 1981): 13, 14.

34. Robert Coles, "Christ and the Poor," *New Oxford Review* 49 (April 1982): 16.

35. See Ronald J. Sider, *Rich Christians in an Age of Hunger* (Downers Grove, Ill.: InterVarsity, 1977), pp. 65-79.

Chapter Ten

1. Kohák, "On the Failure of Marxism," p. 20.

2. Synod of Bishops, November 30, 1971, "Justice in the World," *Official Catholic Teachings: Social Justice*, ed. Vincent P. Mainelli (Wilmington, N.C.: McGrath, 1978), p. 291.

3. Irving Howe, "The Problem of Pornography" [symposium], *Dissent* 25 (Spring 1978): 205.

4. Lasch, *Haven in a Heartless World*, p. 166.

5. Jan Rosenberg, "New Shift in Family Focus?" *Democratic Left* 8 (January 1980): 2, 3.

6. Jane Fonda, as interviewed in Aljean Harmetz, "Fonda at Forty," *McCall's* 105 (January 1978): 126.

7. George F. Will, "Can A Self-Indulgent Society Survive?" *The Wanderer* 113 (September 4, 1980): 126.

8. See interview with Dr. Bernard Nathanson [a founder of the National Abortion Rights Action League], *National Catholic Register* 57 (May 31, 1981): 6.

Chapter Eleven

1. Dorothy Day, *Meditations* (New York: Paulist Press, 1970), pp. 36-37.

From Berkeley to East Berlin and Back

2. G. K. Chesterton, *Orthodoxy* (Garden City, N.Y.: Doubleday Image, 1936), pp. 121, 120.